CHICKEN

◆ *Delicious Creations* ◆

PUBLICATIONS INTERNATIONAL, LTD.

CHICKEN
◆ *Delicious Creations* ◆

BASICS FOR SUCCESS

HELPFUL CHICKEN INFORMATION

Few foods are a better choice for everyday cooking than versatile chicken—good for almost every type of cooking—economical and readily available. Here are some helpful tips for selecting and preparing chicken.

TYPES OF CHICKEN

Chickens are classified by age and weight. Young chickens are tender and cook quickly; older chickens need slow cooking to tenderize them.

Broiler-fryers are young chickens, 7 to 10 weeks old, weighing 1½ to 3½ pounds. The meat is tender, mildly flavored and best when broiled, fried, roasted or sautéed.

Roasters are 16 weeks old and weigh 4 to 6 pounds. They are perfect for roasting and rotisserie cooking.

Capons are young castrated roosters, weighing 5 to 7 pounds. They yield more meat, have a higher fat content and a richer flavor than roasters.

Stewing hens are 1 to 1½ years old, weigh 4½ to 7 pounds and have tough, stringy meat. Stewing hens are excellent for stocks, soups or stews, since moist-heat preparation tenderizes them and enhances their flavor.

WHAT'S AVAILABLE

Supermarkets carry a wide variety of chicken cuts and products. Following are the most popular choices:

Whole chickens are readily available and usually have neck and giblets wrapped separately and stuffed inside.

Cut-up chickens, usually broiler-fryers, are disjointed whole chickens consisting of two breast halves, two thighs, two wings and two drumsticks. Small broiler-fryers also come in halves and quarters.

Chicken pieces are available to suit many needs. Chicken legs are whole broiler-fryer legs with the thighs and drumsticks attached. **Thighs and drumsticks** are cut-apart chicken legs that are packaged separately. **Wings** are also sold separately. **Drumettes** are disjointed wing sections. **Chicken breasts,** popular because of their tender, meaty, sweet character, are available whole or split into halves.

Boneless skinless chicken, which is convenient and quick-cooking, is great for today's busy cook. **Boneless breasts,** also called **cutlets** or **supremes, chicken tenders** and **boneless thighs** are some of the boneless cuts available.

Ground chicken is popular as a low-fat replacement for ground beef or pork. Processed chicken includes **canned chunk chicken, chicken sausage, chicken franks** and traditional **deli** and **luncheon meats.**

STORING CHICKEN

Fresh, raw chicken can be stored in its original wrap safely for up to two days in the coldest part of the refrigerator. Chicken can be frozen in its original packaging safely for up to two months. For longer freezing, double-wrap or rewrap the chicken with freezer paper, aluminum foil or plastic wrap for an airtight package, then label, date and freeze. Store chicken in smaller, meal-size portions to reduce thawing time.

Thaw frozen chicken, wrapped, in the refrigerator. Thawing times vary depending on the size of the chicken pieces and the package. A general guideline is to allow 24 hours thawing time for a 5-pound whole chicken; allow about 5 hours per pound for thawing chicken pieces. Never thaw chicken at room temperature as this promotes bacterial growth.

CHICKEN PREPARATION TIPS

• Before working with raw chicken, cutting board, utensils and hands should be clean. After working with raw chicken, wash cutting boards, knives and hands in hot sudsy water. This eliminates the risk of contaminating other foods with salmonella bacteria that is often present in raw chicken.

• Chicken should always be cooked completely before eating. You should never cook chicken partially, then store it to be finished later, since this promotes bacterial growth.

• Broil chicken 5 to 6 inches from heat and serve immediately for best results.

• To easily cook chicken for use in recipes that call for chopped cooked chicken, microwave 1 pound boneless skinless chicken breasts, covered, at HIGH (100% power) 7 to 8 minutes. If chicken is still pink, microwave at 1 minute intervals until it is no longer pink in center.

• Never let cooked chicken stand at room temperature for more than two hours. In hot weather, reduce the time to one hour.

• About 1¼ pounds of chicken breast meat or a 3-pound broiler-fryer yields about 2 cups chopped cooked chicken.

DONENESS TESTS FOR CHICKEN

Following are several ways to determine if chicken is thoroughly cooked and ready to eat:

• For whole chickens, a meat thermometer inserted into the thickest part of the thigh, but not near the bone or fat, should register 180°F to 185°F before removing the chicken from the oven. If a whole chicken is stuffed, insert the thermometer into the center of the body cavity; when the stuffing registers 165°F, the chicken should be done. (Chicken should be stuffed *just before* roasting.) Roasted whole chicken breasts are done when they register 170°F on a meat thermometer.

• To test bone-in chicken pieces, a fork inserted into the chicken should go in with ease and the juices should run clear. The meat and juices nearest the bone may still be a little pink even though the chicken is cooked thoroughly.

• Boneless chicken pieces are done when the centers are no longer pink; test this by cutting into the chicken with a knife.

LUNCHEON FARE

CHICKEN À LA DIVAN

3 cups cooked fresh broccoli spears
1½ pounds sliced cooked chicken breasts
3 tablespoons FLEISCHMANN'S® Margarine

3 tablespoons all-purpose flour
1½ cups skim milk
½ cup EGG BEATERS® 99% Real Egg Product
2 tablespoons sherry cooking wine
Paprika

Arrange broccoli in the bottom of a 2-quart shallow baking dish or 6 individual baking dishes. Place chicken slices over broccoli; cover with foil. Bake at 350°F for 20 minutes or until hot.

In saucepan, over low heat, melt margarine; blend in flour. Cook, stirring until smooth and bubbly; remove from heat. Gradually stir in milk; return to heat. Heat to a boil, stirring constantly. Gradually blend about half the hot milk mixture into Egg Beaters®, then recombine with remaining hot mixture. Stir in sherry. Spoon sauce over chicken and broccoli; sprinkle lightly with paprika. Serve immediately. *Makes 8 servings*

LEMON-DILLED CHICKEN

2 tablespoons olive oil
2 tablespoons lemon juice
2 cloves garlic, pressed
½ teaspoon dill weed

½ teaspoon salt
2 boneless skinless chicken breasts, halved

Mix oil, lemon juice, garlic, dill weed and salt in small bowl. Place chicken on rack in broiler pan. Brush chicken with lemon mixture. Set oven temperature at broil or 450°F. Position broiler pan about 4 inches from heat; broil 6 to 8 minutes. Turn chicken; broil about 6 to 8 minutes longer or until chicken is golden brown and fork-tender. *Makes 4 servings*

Favorite recipe from **Delmarva Poultry Industry, Inc.**

Chicken à la Divan

Cool and Quick Chinese Chicken Salad

COOL AND QUICK CHINESE CHICKEN SALAD

1 (7-ounce) package
    CREAMETTES® Elbow
    Macaroni (2 cups uncooked)
1½ cups chopped cooked chicken
½ cup thinly sliced carrots
½ cup fresh green beans, cut
    into ½-inch lengths
¼ cup thinly sliced red cabbage

1 (8-ounce) can sliced water
    chestnuts, drained
⅓ cup rice vinegar
⅓ cup tarragon vinegar
⅓ cup sugar
½ teaspoon freshly grated
    ginger root
2 cups torn lettuce

Prepare Creamettes® Elbow Macaroni according to package directions; drain. Combine marcaroni, chicken, carrots, beans, cabbage and water chestnuts. Blend together rice and tarragon vinegars, sugar and ginger root. Toss dressing with salad mixture. Cover and chill. Before serving, toss in lettuce. Refrigerate leftovers. *Makes 6 to 8 servings*

CHICKEN TOSTADAS WITH GRAPE SALSA

CHICKEN MIXTURE

2 cups cubed cooked chicken breasts
½ cup *each* light mayonnaise, chopped celery
2 tablespoons chopped green onions

½ teaspoon ground chili powder
⅛ teaspoon ground cumin
Salt and pepper to taste

GRAPE SALSA

1½ cups California Seedless Grapes, coarsely chopped
¼ cup *each* chopped chives, Anaheim chiles

2 tablespoons *each* chopped cilantro, olive oil
1 tablespoon lemon juice
1 small clove garlic, minced
Salt and pepper to taste

4 tortillas, toasted

Shredded lettuce

For chicken mixture, combine chicken, mayonnaise, celery, onions, chili powder, cumin, salt and pepper; mix thoroughly. Refrigerate until ready to serve.

For Grape Salsa, combine grapes, chives, chiles, cilantro, oil, lemon juice, garlic, salt and pepper; mix well.

To assemble, layer tortillas with lettuce, chicken mixture and Grape Salsa.

Makes 4 servings

Serving Tip: Sprinkle with shredded Cheddar cheese if desired.

Favorite recipe from **California Table Grape Commission**

TAKE-ALONG CHICKEN SALAD

1 tablespoon margarine or butter
2 cups Corn CHEX® brand cereal, crushed to 1 cup
2 tablespoons slivered almonds
2 cups diced cooked chicken
1½ cups diced celery

1 cup (4 ounces) shredded Cheddar cheese
¾ cup sliced pitted ripe olives
¾ cup mayonnaise
¼ cup chopped red pepper
1 teaspoon lemon juice
½ teaspoon seasoned salt
½ teaspoon onion powder

Preheat oven to 350°F. In 2-quart baking dish, melt margarine in oven. Gradually add cereal and nuts, stirring until all pieces are evenly coated. Spread on absorbent paper. In same dish, combine chicken, celery, cheese, olives, mayonnaise, red pepper, lemon juice, seasoned salt and onion powder; mix well. Sprinkle reserved cereal mixture over top. Serve cold or bake 25 to 30 minutes until hot and bubbly. *Makes 4 to 5 servings*

TANGY CHICKEN WALNUT SALAD

1 cup MJB/FARMHOUSE® Long
  Grain White Rice
2 cups chicken broth *or* 2 cups
  water and 2 chicken boullion
  cubes
1 teaspoon butter or margarine

¼ to ½ cup chopped walnuts
2 cups diced cooked chicken
½ cup sliced green onions with
  tops
½ cup sliced celery
¼ cup diced red bell pepper

DRESSING

3 tablespoons olive oil
3 tablespoons lemon juice
1 tablespoon soy sauce

1 teaspoon ginger powder
1 clove garlic, minced

Prepare rice as directed on package using chicken broth instead of water; cool. Heat butter in large skillet over medium-high heat. Sauté walnuts until golden brown; cool. Combine rice, chicken, walnuts, green onions, celery and red pepper in large bowl. Combine oil, lemon juice, soy sauce, ginger and garlic; toss with salad mixture. Refrigerate until ready to serve. Serve chilled.   *Makes about 6 servings*

CHICKEN ITALIAN

1½ cups KELLOGG'S® Corn Flake
  Crumbs
1 cup (8-ounce can) tomato
  sauce
½ teaspoon garlic salt
½ teaspoon dried sweet basil
  leaves, crushed

¼ teaspoon dried oregano
  leaves, crushed
3 pounds boneless skinless
  chicken pieces, washed and
  patted dry
Vegetable cooking spray

1. Place Kellogg's® Corn Flake Crumbs in shallow dish or pan.

2. Combine tomato sauce, garlic salt, basil and oregano. Dip chicken pieces into tomato sauce mixture, then roll in Crumbs.

3. Place chicken pieces, meaty-side up, in shallow pan coated with cooking spray. Do not crowd.

4. Bake at 350°F about 1 hour or until chicken is tender and golden brown. Do not cover pan or turn chicken while baking.   *Makes 8 servings*

Grilled Chicken and Vegetable Sandwiches

GRILLED CHICKEN AND VEGETABLE SANDWICHES

6 tablespoons olive oil
3 cloves garlic
1½ teaspoons ground black
    pepper
1 red or yellow bell pepper,
    halved, cored, seeded, cut
    into ½-inch strips
1 zucchini, cut lengthwise into
    ¼-inch slices
2 COOKIN' GOOD® Boneless
    Skinless Chicken Breasts,
    halved

1 teaspoon salt
1 long loaf Italian bread, cut in
    half lengthwise
1 large tomato, sliced
½ cup loosely packed basil
    leaves or 1 teaspoon dried
    basil leaves, crushed
1 package (8 ounces)
    mozzarella cheese, thinly
    sliced (optional)

1. Prepare outdoor grill for barbecuing. Bring coals to medium heat.

2. In small bowl, combine oil, garlic and black pepper. Place vegetables in center of 12-inch square heavy aluminum foil. Place chicken on platter. Brush vegetables and chicken with olive oil mixture; sprinkle with salt. Fold foil to form packet.

3. Place vegetable packet on barbecue. Grill about 10 minutes or until tender. Remove vegetables; set aside. Grill chicken about 20 minutes, turning once, or until no longer pink.

4. To assemble sandwiches, on bottom half of bread layer peppers, zucchini, chicken, tomato, basil and cheese. Cover with hop half; cut crosswise to make 4 sandwiches. *Makes 4 sandwiches*

Note: For larger quantities multiply ingredients according to servings desired.

Grilled Chicken and Ziti Salad

GRILLED CHICKEN AND ZITI SALAD

1½ pounds COOKIN' GOOD®
   Boneless Skinless Chicken
   Breasts
2 tablespoons fresh lemon juice
1 pound ziti or other tubular
   pasta
   Water
2 large red bell peppers, halved,
   cored, seeded, cut into
   ½-inch pieces
2½ cups thinly sliced celery

1 red onion, thinly sliced
1¼ cups thinly sliced pitted ripe
   olives
¼ cup minced fresh dill
3 tablespoons white wine
   vinegar
2 tablespoons mayonnaise
2 tablespoons Dijon-style
   mustard
   Salt and pepper to taste
⅔ cup olive oil

1. Heat oiled ridged grill pan over medium-high heat *or* set on rack 4 to
6 inches over glowing coals. Grill chicken in pan 8 to 10 minutes on each
side until springy to touch. Transfer to clean shallow dish. Sprinkle
chicken with lemon juice; let cool.

2. Boil ziti in water according to package directions until tender. Rinse ziti in
colander under cold water; drain well.

3. Toss ziti, bell peppers, celery, onion, olives and dill in large bowl. Remove
chicken from bowl, reserving juices. Thinly slice chicken and add to ziti
salad. Add vinegar, mayonnaise, mustard, salt and pepper to juices in
bowl. Whisk mixture well; add oil, whisking until dressing is thoroughly
combined. Add dressing to salad; toss well.   *Makes 8 to 10 servings*

CRISPY CHICKEN DRUMMETTES

CHICKEN DRUMMETTES

2 cups Corn CHEX® brand cereal, crushed to ¾ cup

1 tablespoon dried parsley flakes

¼ teaspoon lemon pepper *or* black pepper

2 tablespoons teriyaki sauce

1½ pounds (about 18) chicken wing drummettes

DIPPING SAUCE*

⅓ cup seedless raspberry jam *or* apricot jam

¼ cup chili sauce

To prepare Chicken Drummettes, preheat oven to 375°F. Lightly grease 13×9×2-inch baking pan. In shallow dish, combine cereal, parsley and pepper; set aside. Place teriyaki sauce in separate shallow dish. Roll drummettes in teriyaki sauce and then cereal mixture. Place drummettes in prepared pan. Bake 40 to 45 minutes until lightly browned.

To prepare Dipping Sauce, in small saucepan over low heat, combine jam and chili sauce; heat until warm.   *Makes about 18 servings*

*Substitute your favorite dipping sauce, such as honey mustard sauce, blue cheese salad dressing, ranch salad dressing, Italian salad dressing, sweet and sour sauce, hot sauce, teriyaki sauce or salsa, if desired.

MICROWAVE DIRECTIONS: To prepare Chicken Drummettes, lightly grease medium microwave-safe baking dish. Follow directions above to prepare Chicken Drummettes. Microwave at MEDIUM-HIGH (70% power) 18 to 20 minutes until done. To prepare Dipping Sauce, in small microwave-safe bowl, combine jam and chili sauce. Microwave on HIGH (100% power) 1 to 1½ minutes until warm.

CHICKEN PASTA SALAD

¾ pound (12 ounces) spiral shape pasta

1¼ cups mayonnaise

1 can (5 fluid ounces) PET® Evaporated Milk

¼ cup Dijon-style mustard

½ teaspoon sugar

½ teaspoon salt

¼ teaspoon pepper

¼ teaspoon ground cumin

2 cups shredded cooked chicken

⅓ cup chopped red onion

½ cup diced celery

½ cup chopped green pepper

Prepare pasta according to package directions; rinse under cold water and drain. In a large bowl, combine mayonnaise, evaporated milk, mustard, sugar, salt, pepper and cumin; mix well. Add chicken, onion, celery, green pepper and drained pasta; mix well. Serve immediately.

Makes 4 main-dish servings

MACARONI AND CHICKEN SALAD

1 (7-ounce) package
  CREAMETTES® Elbow
  Macaroni (2 cups uncooked)
2 cups cubed cooked chicken
1 large apple, cored and diced
1 cup sliced celery
1 cup seedless green grapes,
  halved

1 (15-ounce) can pineapple
  chunks, well drained
1 (11-ounce) can mandarin
  oranges, well drained
½ cup mayonnaise
½ cup sour cream
1 teaspoon sugar
⅛ teaspoon ground nutmeg

Prepare Creamettes® Elbow Macaroni according to package directions; drain. In medium bowl, combine macaroni, chicken, apple, celery, grapes, pineapple and oranges; mix well. In small bowl, blend mayonnaise, sour cream, sugar and nutmeg. Add to salad mixture; toss to coat. Cover; chill thoroughly. Refrigerate leftovers.
Makes 8 to 10 servings

CILANTRO-LIME CHICKEN AND MANGO KABOBS

1 pound boneless skinless
  chicken breasts, cut into
  thin strips
1 large mango, peeled and cut
  into chunks
1 large green pepper, cut into
  1-inch squares
3 tablespoons honey

3 tablespoons lime juice
1 teaspoon grated lime peel
2 tablespoons
  FLEISCHMANN'S® Sweet
  Unsalted Margarine
2 tablespoons chopped cilantro
  or parsley

Thread chicken, mango and pepper alternately on 8 skewers; set aside.

In small saucepan, over medium heat, heat honey, lime juice, lime peel, margarine and cilatro until hot. Keep warm.

Broil or grill kabobs 4 inches from heat for 12 to 15 minutes or until chicken is cooked, turning and brushing with honey mixture often. Reheat any remaining honey mixture to a boil; serve with kabobs.
Makes 8 appetizers or 4 main-dish servings

Macaroni and Chicken Salad

Chicken-Apple Stuffed Pita

CHICKEN-APPLE STUFFED PITA

¼ cup plain lowfat yogurt
2 tablespoons mayonnaise
1 tablespoon honey
2 cups chopped WASHINGTON
   Golden Delicious Apples
1 tablespoon lime juice
1 pound boneless skinless
   chicken breasts, cooked
   and diced

1 cup diced celery
¾ cup chopped unsalted
   peanuts
8 lettuce leaves
4 large pita pocket breads,
   halved

Combine yogurt, mayonnaise and honey in small bowl; set aside. Mix apples with lime juice in large bowl; add chicken, celery and peanuts. Fold yogurt mixture into apple mixture. To serve, place 1 lettuce leaf in each pita half; fill with chicken mixture and serve. *Makes 8 servings*

Favorite recipe from **Washington Apple Commission**

ALL-AMERICAN BARBECUE SAUCE AND MARINADE

¾ cup water
⅔ cup (6-ounce can) CONTADINA® Tomato Paste
⅓ cup loosely packed parsley leaves
¼ cup chopped onion
1 large clove garlic
¼ cup firmly packed dark brown sugar
3 tablespoons apple cider vinegar
1 tablespoon vegetable oil
2 teaspoons Worcestershire sauce
1½ teaspoons prepared mustard
1½ teaspoons salt
2 pounds boneless skinless chicken breasts, halved

In blender container or food processor fitted with metal blade, combine water, tomato paste, parsley, onion, garlic, sugar, vinegar, oil, Worcestershire sauce, mustard and salt. Blend until smooth.

To use as a basting sauce, grill chicken until at least half done before brushing with sauce. Serve any remaining sauce as a table condiment.

To use as a marinade, pour into gallon-size resealable plastic bag. Place chicken in marinade; seal bag. Turn to coat all sides. Refrigerate at least 3 hours or overnight. Remaining marinade should *not* be served as a table condiment. Prepare extra sauce/marinade to serve at the table.

Makes about 2 cups

Note: Sauce may be prepared ahead and refrigerated up to 3 days before use.

Mexican Sauce/Marinade: Follow basic recipe, substituting cilantro leaves for parsley and lemon juice for apple cider vinegar. Add 3 tablespoons chili powder and ½ teaspoon ground cumin.

Oriental Sauce/Marinade: Follow basic recipe, omitting parsley and Worcestershire sauce. Reduce salt to ½ teaspoon. Add ¼ cup soy sauce and 1½ teaspoons ground ginger.

APPLE CHICKEN SALAD

¾ cup mayonnaise
2 tablespoons lemon juice
2 to 3 teaspoons grated ginger root
½ teaspoon salt
¼ teaspoon pepper
3 WASHINGTON Red or Golden Delicious Apples, cored and diced (about 1 pound)
2½ cups (about ¾ pound) diced cooked chicken
¾ cup sliced celery
¼ cup sliced green onions
1 tablespoon chopped cilantro or parsley
Shredded lettuce
Apple slices

Combine mayonnaise, lemon juice, ginger root, salt and pepper; mix well. Combine apples, chicken, celery, green onions and cilantro. Toss apple mixture with dressing; refrigerate at least 1 hour. Serve on lettuce-lined plates. Garnish with apple slices. *Makes 4 to 6 servings*

Favorite recipe from **Washington Apple Commission**

CORN-CRISPED CHICKEN

1 cup KELLOGG'S® Corn Flake Crumbs
1½ teaspoons seasoned salt
3 pounds boneless skinless chicken pieces, washed and patted dry
½ cup evaporated skim milk
Vegetable cooking spray
2 tablespoons margarine, melted

1. Combine Kellogg's® Corn Flake Crumbs and seasoned salt. Dip chicken pieces in evaporated milk and coat with Crumbs mixture. Place in single layer, meaty-side up, in shallow baking pan coated with cooking spray. Drizzle with margarine.

2. Bake in 350°F oven about 1 hour or until chicken is tender and golden brown. Do not cover pan or turn chicken while baking.

Makes 8 servings

CHICKEN TACO SALAD

1 (9-ounce) package ORTEGA® Taco Dinner
¼ cup vegetable oil
¼ cup REGINA® Red Wine Vinegar
8 cups torn lettuce
2 cups cubed cooked chicken
½ cup diced tomato
½ cup peeled and sliced cucumber
¼ cup sliced ripe olives

In small bowl, whisk together taco seasoning mix, taco sauce, oil and vinegar until well blended; set aside.

Line large serving plate with lettuce. Coarsely break taco shells;* arrange on lettuce around outer edge of plate. Toss chicken with ½ cup dressing mixture; spoon over lettuce. Top with tomato, cucumber and olives. Serve with remaining dressing. *Makes 8 servings*

*Taco shells can be heated at 250°F for 5 minutes before breaking.

CHICKEN SUPREME DIJON

1 boneless skinless chicken breast, halved
2 tablespoons BLUE BONNET® Spread, divided
¼ pound fresh mushrooms, sliced
1 medium clove garlic, finely minced

1 tablespoon finely minced onion
1½ cups heavy cream
2 tablespoons GREY POUPON® Dijon Mustard
Cooked wild rice

In skillet, over medium heat, brown chicken in 1 tablespoon spread until done; remove from pan and keep warm.

In same pan, cook mushrooms, garlic and onion in remaining spread until tender. Stir in heavy cream and mustard. Simmer, stirring constantly, until sauce is slightly thickened. Add chicken, turning to coat in sauce. Serve over rice. *Makes 2 servings*

CHICKEN ROTINI STIR-FRY

½ of a (1-pound) package CREAMETTE® Rotini, uncooked
2 tablespoons olive or vegetable oil
2 boneless skinless chicken breasts, cut into strips
1 cup fresh broccoli flowerets
1 cup carrot curls

½ cup sliced red onion
¼ cup water
½ teaspoon chicken-flavor instant bouillon
½ teaspoon dried tarragon leaves, crushed
2 tablespoons grated Parmesan cheese

Prepare Creamette® Rotini according to package directions; drain. In large skillet, heat oil; add chicken, broccoli, carrots and onion. Cook and stir over medium heat until broccoli is tender-crisp. Add water, bouillon and tarragon; cook and stir until chicken is no longer pink. Add hot cooked rotini and Parmesan cheese; toss to coat. Serve immediately. Refrigerate leftovers. *Makes 6 to 8 servings*

WALNUT CHICKEN PINWHEELS

2 boneless skinless chicken
 breasts, halved
12 to 14 spinach leaves
1 package (4 ounces)
 ALOUETTE® with Garlic and
 Spices

5 ounces roasted red peppers,
 sliced *or* 5 ounces pimento
 slices
¾ cup finely chopped California
 walnuts

Pound chicken to about ¼-inch thickness with flat side of meat mallet or chef's knife. Cover each chicken piece with spinach leaves. Spread each with Alouette®. Top with pepper slices and walnuts. Carefully roll up each breast and secure with wooden toothpicks. Bake at 400°F 20 to 25 minutes until cooked through. Chill. Remove toothpicks before serving, then slice into ½-inch rounds. Serve cold.

Makes about 35 appetizers or 8 main-dish servings

TANDOORI CHICKEN KABOBS

6 WAMPLER-LONGACRE®
 Boneless Skinless Chicken
 Breast Halves (about
 1½ pounds)
½ cup plain lowfat yogurt
1 tablespoon peanut oil

1 tablespoon lemon juice
1 teaspoon ground red pepper
½ teaspoon salt
¼ teaspoon paprika
¼ teaspoon ground cinnamon
 Oil for grill (optional)

Cut chicken into 1½-inch cubes. Combine yogurt, oil, lemon juice, red pepper, salt, paprika and cinnamon in large bowl. Coat chicken with yogurt mixture. Refrigerate 2 to 3 hours, stirring once. Meanwhile, soak 6 wooden skewers in water to prevent burning *or* use metal skewers. Lightly oil barbecue grill or spray with nonstick cooking spray. Thread equal amounts of chicken cubes on skewers.

To grill, cook chicken over medium heat about 6 inches from heat, 10 to 15 minutes, turning 3 times, until lightly browned, crisp and cooked through.

Makes 6 servings

TO BROIL: Cook chicken 6 inches from heat, 10 to 15 minutes, turning once.

Prep time: 10 minutes   **Marinating time:** 2 to 3 hours
Cook time: 10 to 15 minutes

Walnut Chicken Pinwheels

CHINESE CHICKEN SALAD WITH CHILEAN GRAPES

4 cups shredded cooked chicken
1 head lettuce, thinly shredded
2 cups imported Chilean red or green grapes, halved or whole and seeded
4 green onions, thinly sliced
1 bunch cilantro or parsley, chopped (reserve a few leaves for garnish)
1 cup chopped peanuts, cashews or slivered almonds
¼ cup toasted sesame seeds
Lemon Dressing (recipe follows)
3 cups bean threads or rice sticks, fried in vegetable or sesame oil* or cooked white rice
1 carrot, thinly sliced on diagonal
Additional whole nuts (optional)
Small clusters of grapes

Mix together chicken, lettuce, grapes, onions, cilantro, nuts and sesame seeds; set aside. Prepare Lemon Dressing; pour over chicken mixture. Toss to coat completely. Place bean threads on 4 to 6 individual serving plates, forming nest. Spoon chicken mixture over bean threads. Garnish with reserved cilantro leaves, a few carrot slices and additional nuts. Place small clusters of grapes on each plate beside salad.   *Makes 4 to 6 servings*

*Deep fry bean threads or rice sticks, a bunch at a time, until light and puffy. Do not burn. Drain on paper towels.

LEMON DRESSING: Blend together 1 teaspoon sugar and ½ teaspoon dry mustard; stir in ¼ cup sesame oil or salad oil, 3 tablespoons lemon juice, 1 minced clove fresh garlic and 1 teaspoon soy sauce.

Favorite recipe from **Chilean Fresh Fruit Association**

CHICKEN PAGODA SALAD

2 cups shredded cooked chicken (about 8 ounces)
¼ cup vegetable oil
¼ cup REGINA® Red Wine Vinegar
3 tablespoons soy sauce
1 tablespoon honey
2 cloves garlic, crushed
6 cups torn mixed salad greens
½ pint cherry tomatoes, halved
1 (8-ounce) can sliced water chestnuts, drained
Chow mein noodles, for garnish

In large bowl, combine chicken, oil, vinegar, soy sauce, honey and garlic; let stand 15 minutes. Add salad greens, tomatoes and water chestnuts, tossing to coat well. Cover; chill until serving time. Serve with chow mein noodles if desired.   *Makes 6 servings*

Oriental Chicken Salad

ORIENTAL CHICKEN SALAD

1 pound COOKIN' GOOD®
    Boneless Skinless Chicken
    Breast Halves (about 3)
  Water
¼ cup lite soy sauce
1 tablespoon white vinegar
1 tablespoon sesame oil
1 clove garlic, crushed
¾ teaspoon ground ginger

¼ pound snow peas, trimmed,
    parboiled 1 to 2 minutes
1 red bell pepper, halved, cored,
    seeded, cut into 2×¼-inch
    strips
2 carrots, cut diagonally into
    ¼-inch slices, parboiled 3 to
    5 minutes
3 green onions, cut diagonally
    into 1-inch slices

1. Place chicken in 10-inch skillet; add water to cover. Bring to a boil over high heat. Reduce heat to low. Cover; simmer 15 to 20 minutes until chicken is tender and juices run clear when pierced with a fork. Drain; cut into small bite-size pieces when cool enough to handle. Set aside.

2. Combine soy sauce, vinegar, sesame oil, garlic and ginger in medium nonmetallic bowl. Add chicken; toss together until well combined. Cover; refrigerate at least 2 hours, stirring occasionally.

3. Add snow peas, red pepper, carrots and green onions; toss to coat with marinade. Serve or refrigerate. *Makes 4 to 6 servings*

PECAN-COATED WINGETTES

WINGETTES

6 tablespoons Dijon-style
   mustard
4 tablespoons butter, melted
2 cups pecans

⅓ cup plain bread crumbs
12 COOKIN' GOOD® Chicken
   Wingettes, thawed

DIPPING SAUCE

½ cup sour cream
½ cup plain yogurt
2 tablespoons Dijon-style
   mustard

2 tablespoons minced onion or
   minced green onions
⅛ to ¼ teaspoon hot pepper
   sauce

1. Preheat oven to 375°F. Combine 6 tablespoons mustard and butter in bowl; set aside.

2. Place pecans and bread crumbs in food processor bowl. Process until pecans are finely chopped. Place pecan mixture on waxed paper or in pie plate. Dip chicken in mustard mixture to coat, then in pecan mixture. Arrange Wingettes on baking sheet. Bake 25 minutes or until fork-tender.

3. While chicken is baking, whisk sour cream, yogurt, 2 tablespoons mustard, onion and hot pepper sauce in bowl. Serve Wingettes with Dipping Sauce. *Makes 4 to 6 servings*

ZESTY CHICKEN EN PAPILLOTE

2 boneless skinless chicken
   breasts, halved
1 package ALOUETTE® Light
   Soft Spreadable Cheese

1 red pepper, julienned
1 zucchini, julienned
4 mushrooms, sliced

1. Fold four 18×18-inch pieces of parchment paper or foil in half; cut into shape of a half heart (when unfolded whole heart is formed).

2. Cut chicken into strips; place ½ breast on 1 side of heart. Top chicken with 3 tablespoons cheese and ¼ of *each* vegetable. Fold other half of heart over to enclose chicken-cheese mixture; fold edges to seal. Repeat process with remaining chicken, cheese, vegetables and parchment.

3. Place packages on cookie sheet; bake in preheated 400°F oven 10 to 12 minutes. Place packages on plate. Serve letting diner open to release smell and flavor at table. *Makes 4 servings*

Pecan-Coated Wingettes

HAWAIIAN CHICKEN SALAD

4 cups chopped cooked chicken
1 can (8 ounces) crushed pineapple in natural juice, drained
1 small apple, chopped
1 rib celery, chopped
1 small onion, chopped
½ cup chopped green bell pepper

1 cup mayonnaise
¼ teaspoon salt
¼ teaspoon ground ginger
2 cups HONEY ALMOND DELIGHT® brand cereal, crushed to 1 cup
1 tablespoon margarine or butter, melted

Preheat oven to 350°F. In 1½-quart baking dish, combine chicken, pineapple, apple, celery, onion and green pepper. In small bowl, combine mayonnaise, salt and ginger. Add to chicken mixture, stirring until well combined. In separate small bowl, combine cereal and margarine. Sprinkle evenly over chicken. Bake 25 to 30 minutes until hot. *Makes 6 servings*

Note: Salad is also delicious served cold, unbaked.

MICROWAVE DIRECTIONS: Follow directions above using 1½-quart microwave-safe baking dish; *EXCEPT* do not sprinkle cereal onto chicken mixture prior to initial cooking. Microwave on HIGH (100% power), covered, 4 minutes; stir. Sprinkle cereal evenly over chicken mixture. Microwave on HIGH 2 to 2½ minutes until hot.

TARRAGON CHICKEN BURGERS

3 tablespoons olive oil, divided
¼ cup finely chopped onion
1 small clove garlic, finely chopped
1 pound WAMPLER-LONGACRE® Ground Chicken
2 tablespoons chopped fresh parsley

1 teaspoon dried tarragon leaves, crushed
¼ teaspoon dried thyme leaves, crushed
¼ teaspoon salt
⅛ teaspoon freshly ground pepper
2 tablespoons all-purpose flour

Heat 1 tablespoon olive oil in skillet over medium-low heat. Add onion and garlic; cook until tender and soft, about 3 minutes. Meanwhile, combine chicken, parsley, tarragon, thyme, salt and pepper in mixing bowl. Blend onion mixture with chicken mixture. Form into 4 patties; dust with flour. Heat remaining 2 tablespoons olive oil in clean skillet over medium heat. Cook until patties are browned on both sides, no pink remains in center and juices run clear. *Makes 4 servings*

Prep time: about 7 minutes   **Cook time:** about 5 minutes

California Date-Chicken Salad

CALIFORNIA DATE-CHICKEN SALAD

2 oranges, peeled
8 cups mixed salad greens, washed
1¾ cups shredded cooked boneless skinless chicken breast
¾ cup pitted California dates, sliced
½ cup coarsely chopped toasted walnuts
⅓ cup crumbled blue cheese
3 tablespoons olive oil
1 tablespoon balsamic or red wine vinegar
Salt and black pepper to taste

Slice oranges crosswise into ¼-inch slices; cut into quarters. Toss oranges, salad greens, chicken, dates, walnuts and blue cheese in large bowl. Whisk together olive oil and vinegar. Toss dressing in with salad until lightly coated. Season to taste with salt and pepper.

Makes 2 servings or 4 appetizer servings

Favorite recipe from **California Date Administrative Committee**

FESTIVE ENTERTAINING

GRILLED CHICKEN AND APPLE WITH FRESH ROSEMARY

½ cup apple juice
¼ cup white wine vinegar
¼ cup vegetable oil or light olive oil
1 tablespoon chopped fresh rosemary *or* 1 teaspoon dried rosemary leaves, crushed

¼ teaspoon salt
¼ teaspoon ground black pepper
3 boneless skinless chicken breasts, halved
2 WASHINGTON Golden Delicious Apples, cored and sliced into ½-inch-thick rings

1. Combine juice, vinegar, oil, rosemary, salt and pepper in shallow baking dish or bowl. Add chicken and apples; marinate in refrigerator at least 30 minutes.

2. Heat grill. Remove chicken and apples from marinade; arrange on hot grill. Discard marinade. Cook chicken 20 minutes or until cooked through, turning to grill both sides. Cook and turn apples about 6 minutes or until crisp-tender. Serve.   *Makes 6 servings*

Favorite recipe from **Washington Apple Commission**

DIJON ALMOND CHICKEN

2 tablespoons BLUE BONNET® Spread, melted
2 tablespoons GREY POUPON® Country Dijon Mustard

2 boneless skinless chicken breasts, halved
½ cup chopped almonds

In small bowl, combine spread and mustard. Dip chicken breast in mustard mixture and then coat with chopped almonds. Place into 10×6×1¾-inch greased baking dish.

Bake at 375°F for about 30 minutes or until done.   *Makes 4 servings*

Grilled Chicken and Apple
with Fresh Rosemary

Orange Glazed Chicken and Squash Bake

ORANGE GLAZED CHICKEN AND SQUASH BAKE

4 broiler-fryer chicken legs	½ cup orange marmalade
½ teaspoon salt	1 tablespoon lemon juice
¼ teaspoon pepper	1 teaspoon grated lemon peel
2 small acorn squash, quartered lengthwise	¼ teaspoon ground nutmeg
	¼ teaspoon ground cinnamon

Place chicken in single layer on wire rack in large shallow baking pan. Sprinkle salt and pepper over chicken. Place squash in medium baking dish. Add water to cover bottom of dish; cover with foil.

Bake chicken and squash in 375°F oven 25 minutes. Mix marmalade, lemon juice and peel, nutmeg and cinnamon in small bowl. Brush marmalade mixture over chicken. Bake 20 minutes longer. Remove cover from squash. Brush remaining marmalade mixture over chicken and squash. Bake 10 minutes more or until chicken and squash are fork-tender.

Makes 4 servings

Favorite recipe from **Delmarva Poultry Industry, Inc.**

SAUTÉED BANANAS WITH EXOTIC CHICKEN

4 boneless skinless chicken breasts, cut into bite-size pieces
Salt and pepper to taste
2 teaspoons vegetable oil, divided
1 medium onion, halved, thinly sliced
2 cans (10½ ounces *each*) chicken broth
1¼ cups converted rice
⅓ cup DOLE® Chopped Dates
⅓ cup orange marmalade

2 tablespoons *each* lemon juice, tomato paste
1½ teaspoons *each* garlic powder, dried coriander leaves, crushed
½ teaspoon *each* ground red pepper, salt
1 medium DOLE® Carrot, grated (½ cup)
3 green-tip, medium DOLE® Bananas, peeled
⅓ cup DOLE® Pistachios or Almonds, chopped
⅓ cup chopped cilantro

• Season chicken with salt and pepper. Heat 1 teaspoon oil in large nonstick skillet over medium-high heat. Stir-fry chicken until lightly browned. Stir in onion. Reduce heat to low. Cook 2 minutes.

• Stir in broth, rice, dates, marmalade, lemon juice, tomato paste, garlic powder, coriander, red pepper and salt. Bring to a boil. Reduce heat to low. Cover and simmer 25 minutes or until rice is done and liquid is absorbed. Remove from heat; stir in carrot.

• Cut bananas in half crosswise, then lengthwise to make 12 pieces. Heat remaining oil in nonstick skillet. Cook bananas until lightly browned.

• Serve chicken and rice with bananas. Sprinkle with pistachios and cilantro.

Makes 6 servings

Prep time: 20 minutes   **Cook time:** 35 minutes

FRIED CHICKEN

1 can (12 fluid ounces) PET® Evaporated Milk
1 egg
1 cup flour
1 teaspoon salt
½ teaspoon pepper

½ teaspoon garlic powder
Oil for frying
1 broiler-fryer chicken, cut into serving pieces (3 to 3½ pounds)

In a bowl, combine evaporated milk and egg. In separate bowl, combine flour, salt, pepper and garlic powder. In large skillet, heat oil on medium-high heat. Dip chicken pieces in evaporated milk and egg mixture, then coat with flour mixture. Fry in hot oil turning frequently until done, about 35 to 40 minutes.

Makes 4 servings

CHICKEN ROYALE

2 boneless skinless chicken
   breasts, halved
1 package (4 ounces) Boursin or
   other herb-flavored cheese,
   quartered
½ cup English walnuts, finely
   chopped
4 large spinach leaves, steamed
   slightly
½ teaspoon salt
½ teaspoon pepper
½ cup dry white wine
½ cup bottled reduced-calorie
   raspberry vinaigrette
   dressing*
2 tablespoons margarine
   Hot cooked rice

Pound chicken breasts to ¼-inch thickness with flat side of meat mallet or chef's knife. Roll cheese in walnuts. Place 1 spinach leaf on each breast; top with a cheese quarter. Fold chicken around spinach and cheese to form a mound. Sprinkle salt and pepper over chicken. Place chicken in baking pan. Cover; bake in 350°F oven 30 minutes or until chicken is fork-tender.

Mix wine and dressing in small skillet. Cook over medium heat until sauce is reduced by one-half; stir in margarine. Pour sauce over chicken. Serve with rice.   *Makes 4 servings*

*If raspberry vinaigrette dressing is not available, substitute ¼ cup bottled reduced-calorie red wine vinegar and oil dressing and ¼ cup seedless raspberry jam. Omit margarine.

Favorite recipe from **Delmarva Poultry Industry, Inc.**

SESAME SEED CHICKEN

1 cup KELLOGG'S® Corn Flake
   Crumbs
3 tablespoons sesame seeds
1 egg
½ cup skim milk
½ cup all-purpose flour
1½ teaspoons ground ginger
¼ teaspoon salt
3 pounds broiler chicken pieces
   (without or with skin),
   washed and patted dry
   Vegetable cooking spray

1. Combine Kellogg's® Corn Flake Crumbs and sesame seeds. Set aside in shallow dish or pan.

2. In second shallow dish or pan, beat egg and milk slightly. Add flour, ginger and salt. Mix until smooth. Dip chicken into batter. Coat with crumbs mixture. Place in single layer, meaty-side up, in shallow baking pan coated with cooking spray.

3. Bake at 350°F about 1 hour or until chicken is tender and done.
                                          Makes 8 servings

Chicken Royale

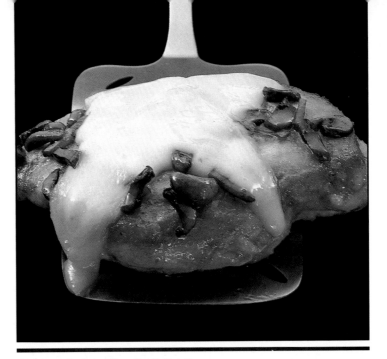

Chicken Cutlets Classica® Fontina

CHICKEN CUTLETS CLASSICA® FONTINA

4 tablespoons butter, divided
8 ounces fresh mushrooms, cut
    into slivers
4 boneless skinless chicken
    breasts, halved
Flour for coating

    Ground pepper
⅓ cup dry white wine
2 tablespoons Madeira or sherry
4 ounces CLASSICA® Fontina,
    cut into 8 slices

Preheat oven to 350°F. Heat 2 tablespoons butter in large skillet over medium heat; cook mushrooms until tender. Remove mushrooms; set aside. Remove liquid from skillet; reserve.

Roll chicken in flour to coat. Season with pepper. Heat remaining 2 tablespoons butter in skillet over medium heat; brown chicken, turning once. Remove chicken; place in 9-inch square baking dish. Sprinkle with mushrooms; set aside.

Add white wine and Madeira to skillet. Bring to a boil, stirring constantly. Reduce heat to low. Cook until liquid is reduced by half, about 5 minutes. Pour wine mixture over chicken.

Bake until chicken is no longer pink, about 20 minutes. Place slice of Classica® Fontina on each chicken breast. Return to oven. Bake until cheese is melted, about 3 to 5 minutes. *Makes 6 to 8 servings*

APRICOT GLAZED CHICKEN

1 jar (12 ounces) apricot
    preserves
2 tablespoons reduced-fat
    mayonnaise
1 tablespoon ketchup
¼ teaspoon dry mustard
8 boneless skinless chicken
    breasts (about 2 pounds)
2 tablespoons margarine
½ cup finely chopped onion
½ cup finely chopped celery

½ cup thinly sliced mushrooms
1¼ cups KELLOGG'S®
    ALL-BRAN® cereal
½ cup chicken broth
1 can (8 ounces) water
    chestnuts, drained and
    chopped
½ teaspoon salt
¼ teaspoon pepper
¼ teaspoon rubbed sage
    Hot cooked rice

1. Combine preserves, mayonnaise, ketchup and dry mustard. Set aside for sauce.

2. Place each chicken breast between 2 pieces of waxed paper. Pound with flat side of meat mallet or chef's knife to ⅛-inch thickness, being careful not to tear meat. Set aside.

3. Melt margarine in medium skillet. Add onion and celery. Stirring frequently, cook over medium heat until crisp-tender. Stir in mushrooms and cook 3 to 4 minutes longer.

4. Combine Kellogg's® All-Bran® cereal and chicken broth. Let stand about 1 minute or until cereal absorbs broth. Mix in vegetables, water chestnuts, salt, pepper and sage. Top each breast with ¼ cup filling. Roll, folding in ends. Place breasts seam-side down into a 12×8-inch shallow baking dish. Cover chicken rolls with reserved sauce.

5. Bake uncovered at 350°F about 45 minutes or until chicken is tender and done. Serve over hot rice if desired. *Makes 8 servings*

HONEY-MUSTARD GLAZED CHICKEN

½ cup GREY POUPON® Dijon or
    Country Dijon Mustard
¼ cup honey
2 tablespoons lemon juice
1 clove garlic, crushed

¼ teaspoon dried tarragon
    leaves, crushed
1 broiler-fryer chicken, cut into
    serving pieces (3 pounds)
    Fresh tarragon sprigs, for
    garnish

In small bowl, combine mustard, honey, lemon juice, garlic and tarragon. Grill or broil chicken 45 minutes or until done, turning occasionally and brushing with mustard mixture frequently. Arrange on serving platter; garnish with fresh tarragon if desired. *Makes 4 servings*

GRILLED ROSEMARY CHICKEN

3 large cloves garlic, quartered
3 tablespoons olive oil
3 tablespoons Dijon-style
    mustard
2 tablespoons lemon juice
2 tablespoons fresh rosemary,
    minced *or* 2 teaspoons
    dried rosemary leaves,
    crumbled

1 teaspoon ground black pepper
1 COOKIN' GOOD® Broiler
    Chicken, cut into serving
    pieces (about 3½ pounds)

1. Combine garlic, oil, mustard and lemon juice in blender. Blend until smooth and creamy. Pour mixture into bowl; stir in rosemary and pepper. Brush chicken pieces with mustard mixture. Cover; refrigerate 6 hours or overnight.

2. Prepare outdoor grill for barbecuing. Bring coals to medium heat. Place chicken, meaty-side up, on grill. Cook 12 minutes. Turn; continue to cook 20 to 25 minutes until chicken is no longer pink. Remove to clean plate.

Makes 4 to 6 servings

TO BROIL: Preheat broiler; arrange chicken on rack in broiling pan. Broil 7 to 9 inches from heat 25 minutes. Turn; continue broiling 20 minutes or until chicken is no longer pink.

DOUBLE-COATED CHICKEN

7 cups KELLOGG'S® CORN
    FLAKES® cereal, crushed
    to 1¾ cups
1 egg
1 cup skim milk
1 cup all-purpose flour
½ teaspoon salt

¼ teaspoon black pepper
3 pounds broiler chicken pieces
    (without or with skin),
    washed and patted dry
3 tablespoons margarine,
    melted

1. Measure crushed Kellogg's® Corn Flakes cereal into shallow dish or pan. Set aside.

2. In small mixing bowl, beat egg and milk slightly. Add flour, salt and pepper. Mix until smooth. Dip chicken in batter. Coat with cereal. Place in single layer, meaty-side up, in foil-lined shallow baking pan. Drizzle with margarine.

3. Bake at 350°F about 1 hour or until chicken is tender and done. Do not cover pan or turn chicken while baking.

Makes 8 servings

Grilled Rosemary Chicken

Southwestern Grilled Chicken with Yogurt Salsa

SOUTHWESTERN GRILLED CHICKEN WITH YOGURT SALSA

1 container (8 ounces) plain
    lowfat yogurt
2 cans (4 ounces *each*) sliced
    mild green chilies, drained
¼ cup minced green onions
1 teaspoon ground cumin
1 teaspoon salt

1 pound boneless skinless
    chicken breasts, halved
1 *each* red, green and yellow
    bell pepper, *each* cut into
    sixths
1 tablespoon reduced-calorie
    mayonnaise

Combine yogurt, green chilies, green onions, cumin and salt in medium bowl. Set aside ⅔ cup yogurt mixture for Yogurt Salsa; refrigerate. Pierce chicken liberally on both sides with fork tines; add to bowl with yogurt mixture, turning to coat both sides. Marinate 15 minutes.

To cook over coals, place chicken and peppers on rack 3 to 4 inches away from medium-hot coals. Grill, turning once, until chicken is cooked through and peppers are crisp-tender, about 10 minutes.

Meanwhile, prepare Yogurt Salsa by stirring mayonnaise into reserved ⅔ cup yogurt mixture; place in small serving bowl.

To serve, slice each breast into ½-inch-thick slices. Arrange chicken and peppers on individual plates. Serve with Yogurt Salsa and kidney beans with corn kernels in lettuce cups, if desired. *Makes 4 servings*

TO BROIL: Place chicken and peppers on rack in broiler pan 4 to 5 inches away from preheated broiler. Cook following directions for grilling.

Favorite recipe from **National Dairy Board**

CHICKEN WITH SWEET AND SOUR GRAPE SAUCE

1 pound boneless skinless
    chicken
1 egg, beaten
½ cup corn flake crumbs
    Salt and pepper
1 tablespoon vegetable oil
½ cup sliced onion

1 cup red pepper strips
1 tablespoon *each* soy sauce,
    finely minced fresh ginger
    root
¼ cup apricot preserves
1 cup California Seedless
    Grapes

Cut chicken into bite-size pieces; dip into egg. Mix corn flake crumbs with salt and pepper; coat chicken with crumbs. Place on greased baking sheet; bake at 375°F 15 minutes or until golden. Arrange on serving platter. Heat oil in skillet over medium-high heat; cook onion until soft. Add pepper strips, soy sauce and ginger root; cook 1 minute. Stir in preserves and grapes; cook until heated through. Pour over chicken pieces.

Makes about 4 servings

Tip: Frozen prepared breaded chicken nuggets can be used instead of breading your own chicken pieces.

Favorite recipe from **California Table Grape Commission**

APPLE & RICE-STUFFED CHICKEN

1 package LIPTON® Golden
    Sauté Rice Mix—Oriental
    Style
3 cups water, divided
1 tart cooking apple, diced
½ cup finely chopped celery

2 boneless skinless chicken
    breasts, halved (about
    1 pound), pounded to
    ¼ inch thick
Paprika

Preheat oven to 350°F.

In medium saucepan, bring Oriental style rice mix, 2½ cups water, apple and celery to a boil. Reduce heat and simmer uncovered, stirring occasionally, 10 minutes; let cool slightly.

Evenly spread each chicken breast with ¼ cup rice mixture; bring up sides to form bundles and secure with wooden toothpicks.

In 11×7-inch baking dish, combine remaining rice mixture with remaining ½ cup water. Arrange chicken bundles over rice. Sprinkle with paprika. Bake 25 minutes or until chicken is tender and done. Remove toothpicks before serving.

Makes 4 servings

HOLLYWOOD CHICKEN

1 COOKIN' GOOD Roaster
   Chicken (about 5 to
   7 pounds)
1 small orange, quartered
1 small onion, quartered
4 sprigs fresh cilantro
2¾ teaspoons salt, divided
  ½ teaspoon freshly ground black
   pepper
  ¼ cup butter or margarine,
   melted, divided
1 cup orange juice

  ½ cup loosely packed fresh
   cilantro leaves
  ¼ cup orange marmalade
  ½ teaspoon grated orange peel
   Liquid red pepper seasoning,
   to taste
1 tablespoon flour
   Orange segments and
   avocado slices (optional)
   Fresh sprigs of cilantro
   (optional)

1. Rinse Roaster with cold water and drain well; pat dry with paper towels. Loosely stuff cavity of roaster with orange, onion and cilantro sprigs. Preheat oven to 375°F. Sprinkle bird inside and out with 2½ teaspoons salt and pepper. Skewer Roaster openings, truss wings underneath body and tie drumsticks together. Place breast side up on rack in shallow open roasting pan. Brush with 1 tablespoon butter; set aside.

2. Combine orange juice, cilantro leaves, orange marmalade, remaining 3 tablespoons butter, remaining ¼ teaspoon salt, orange peel and pepper seasoning in container of food processor or blender. Process until well blended and smooth; set aside 1¼ cups. Bake Roaster in preheated oven 2 hours or about 20 minutes per pound, basting occasionally with remaining orange mixture, until meat thermometer registers 185°F, leg moves freely or juices run clear when pierced with a fork. Let Roaster stand 20 minutes while completing sauce.

3. Remove 1 tablespoon drippings from roasting pan to small saucepan. Whisk in 1 tablespoon flour and cook over medium heat 3 minutes, stirring constantly. Gradually whisk in reserved basting liquid, stirring constantly until thickened. (If mixture is too thick, add additional orange juice until desired consistency.) Garnish with orange, avocado and cilantro.

Makes 5 to 7 servings

Note: If Roaster skin begins to brown too much, cover brown areas with foil.

Hollywood Chicken

COUNTRY FRENCH CHICKEN BREASTS

1 tablespoon butter or
  margarine
2 boneless skinless chicken
  breasts, halved (about
  1 pound)
1 cup water

1 envelope LIPTON® Recipe
  Secrets™ Savory Herb with
  Garlic Recipe Soup Mix
1 tablespoon lemon juice
4 lemon slices
  Hot cooked rice

In 12-inch skillet, melt butter over medium heat and add chicken, browning
2 minutes on each side. Stir in water, savory herb with garlic recipe soup
mix and lemon juice; arrange lemon slices on chicken. Simmer, covered,
10 minutes or until sauce is thickened slightly and chicken is done. To serve,
arrange chicken over hot rice and spoon sauce over chicken.

Makes about 4 servings

CHICKEN BREASTS IN
ORANGE-MUSTARD SAUCE

6 boneless skinless chicken
  breasts, halved
1½ teaspoons dried rosemary
  leaves, crushed
1½ teaspoons dried oregano
  leaves, crushed
1 teaspoon paprika
1 teaspoon salt

½ teaspoon ground black pepper
⅔ cup GREY POUPON® Country
  Dijon Mustard
1 (6-ounce) container frozen
  orange juice concentrate,
  thawed
  Orange twists, for garnish

Pound each chicken breast to ½-inch thickness with flat side of meat mallet
or chef's knife and place in single layer in large baking pan; set aside.

Blend rosemary, oregano, paprika, salt and pepper; sprinkle evenly over
chicken, turning to coat both sides. Cover pan with foil. Bake at 400°F for
20 to 25 minutes. Pour off any excess fat.

In small bowl, blend mustard and orange juice concentrate; pour over
chicken, turning to coat both sides. Cover pan. Bake 10 minutes more or
until chicken is done.

To serve, place one chicken breast on each dinner plate; top with 1 to 2
ounces pan juices. Garnish with orange twist; serve immediately.

Makes 12 servings

CALAMATA CHICKEN CUTLETS WITH PASTA

2 tablespoons olive oil
2 cloves garlic, minced
2 boneless skinless chicken
    breasts, cubed
½ red bell pepper, chopped
1 small onion, chopped
12 Calamata olives

1 can (8 ounces) DEL MONTE®
    Zucchini with Italian-Style
    Tomato Sauce
½ pound pasta, cooked
2 ounces goat cheese, crumbled
    Chopped parsley

Heat oil in heavy skillet over medium-high heat; sauté garlic 2 minutes. Add chicken; sauté on all sides. Add pepper, onion and olives; cook 3 minutes. Add Zucchini with Italian-Style Tomato Sauce; heat through. Serve over hot cooked pasta. Top with goat cheese and parsley.   *Makes 2 servings*

Helpful Hint: Use pasta of your choice. If Calamata olives are not available, use other Italian or ripe olives.

SPICY PINEAPPLE CHICKEN

1 teaspoon vegetable oil
6 skinless chicken thighs
6 large cloves garlic, chopped
1 can (20 ounces) DOLE®
    Crushed Pineapple in Juice
⅓ cup light soy sauce
¼ cup honey

3 to 4 tablespoons cider vinegar
¼ teaspoon pepper
3 medium DOLE® Carrots, thinly
    sliced
½ medium DOLE® Red Bell
    Pepper, cut in strips
3 cups hot cooked rice

• In large nonstick skillet heat oil over medium-high heat; brown chicken on one side. Sprinkle with garlic. Turn chicken and brown other side.

• Combine undrained pineapple, soy sauce, honey, vinegar and pepper. Add to skillet. Bring to a boil. Reduce heat. Cover and simmer 15 minutes.

• With slotted spoon, remove chicken to platter. Boil sauce over high heat 3 to 5 minutes to reduce and thicken. Add carrots and bell pepper. Reduce heat. Cover; cook 3 to 5 minutes until vegetables are crisp-tender.

• Spoon vegetables and sauce over chicken and rice.   *Makes 6 servings*

Prep time: 20 minutes   **Cook time:** 30 minutes

GINGER CHICKEN ON SKEWERS

⅓ cup soy sauce
3 green onions, diced
2 tablespoons minced fresh
  ginger
2 tablespoons orange juice
1 tablespoon vegetable oil or
  sesame oil

2 pounds COOKIN' GOOD®
  Tenderloins of Chicken
  Breast, thawed
1 large red pepper, cut into
  28 pieces
1 large green pepper, cut into
  28 pieces

1. Combine soy sauce, green onions, ginger, orange juice and oil in large bowl. Add chicken tenders; toss until coated with marinade. Cover; refrigerate 2 hours.

2. Meanwhile, soak 28 wooden skewers (8 inches *each*) in water to prevent burning *or* use metal skewers.

3. Thread 2 pieces of pepper (1 red and 1 green) and 1 chicken tender on each skewer. Arrange filled skewers on broiler racks. Broil 4 inches from heat 6 minutes, turning once, or until chicken is no longer pink.

Makes 14 servings (2 filled skewers per person)

ROLLED CHICKEN DIJON

3 boneless skinless chicken
  breasts, halved (about
  1½ pounds)
½ cup GREY POUPON® Country
  Dijon Mustard

¼ cup finely chopped green
  onions
2 tablespoons BLUE BONNET®
  Spread, melted
1 teaspoon dried tarragon
  leaves, crushed

Pound chicken pieces to ½-inch thickness with flat side of meat mallet or chef's knife; set aside.

In small bowl, blend mustard, green onions, spread and tarragon. Brush about 1 tablespoon mustard mixture on each chicken piece. Roll up; secure with wooden toothpicks if necessary. Place in baking dish; brush with mustard mixture. Bake at 375°F for 25 to 30 minutes, brushing occasionally with remaining mustard mixture. Remove toothpicks before serving.

Makes 6 servings

Pecan Country Chicken

PECAN COUNTRY CHICKEN

2 boneless skinless chicken
   breasts, halved
¾ teaspoon salt
½ teaspoon freshly ground
   pepper
2 tablespoons butter
8 ounces fresh mushrooms,
   chopped
½ small onion, diced *or* 6 green
   onions, diced
4 ounces cream cheese,
   softened

1 tablespoon French-style
   mustard
1 tablespoon snipped fresh
   thyme *or* 1 teaspoon dried
   thyme leaves, crushed
1½ cups finely diced Texas
   Pecans
1 cup fine bread crumbs
¼ cup minced fresh parsley
½ cup butter, melted
   Hot cooked rice

Pound chicken breasts to ¼-inch thickness with flat side of meat mallet or chef's knife. Sprinkle with salt and pepper. Heat 2 tablespoons butter in skillet over medium-high heat. Cook mushrooms and onion until onion is soft. Cool mixture before combining with cream cheese, mustard and thyme.

Divide cream cheese mixture into 4 equal portions; spread 1 portion on each piece of chicken. Fold over ends and roll up, pressing edges to seal. Mix pecans, bread crumbs and parsley in bowl. Dip chicken into ½ cup butter, then into crumbs, turning to coat. Place on greased baking sheet, seam side down. Bake at 350°F 35 minutes or until chicken is no longer pink in center. Serve with rice. *Makes 4 servings*

Favorite recipe from **Pecan Marketing Board**

PINEAPPLE CHICKEN RICE BOWL

3 boneless skinless chicken breasts, cut into bite-size pieces
½ cup light soy sauce
¼ cup sherry
4 DOLE® Green Onions, thinly sliced, divided
2 tablespoons honey
1 medium DOLE® Fresh Pineapple
18 bamboo skewers (6 inches each), soaked in water

3 cups DOLE® Broccoli florettes, cooked
1 small DOLE® Red Bell Pepper, cut into strips
2 medium DOLE® Carrots, grated (1 cup)
¼ cup DOLE® Chopped Almonds, toasted
6 cups hot cooked brown rice
Seasoned rice vinegar (optional)

• Marinate chicken in mixture of soy sauce, sherry, half the green onions and honey. Refrigerate 15 minutes or longer.

• Twist crown from pineapple. Cut pineapple in half lengthwise. Refrigerate half for another use. Cut fruit from shell. Cut into chunks. Thread pineapple and chicken onto skewers. Grill or broil 4 inches from heat source 6 to 8 minutes, turning and basting with marinade.

• Combine broccoli, red pepper, carrots, almonds and remaining 2 green onions. Spoon hot rice into individual bowls. Spoon on broccoli mixture; sprinkle with vinegar. Spoon on Celery Sauce. Serve with filled skewers.

Makes 6 servings

CELERY SAUCE

½ cup minced DOLE® Celery
½ cup reduced fat mayonnaise
2 tablespoons light soy sauce

1 tablespoon seasoned rice vinegar

Combine celery, mayonnaise, soy sauce and vinegar.

Prep time: 25 minutes   **Marinating time:** 15 minutes
Cook time: 15 minutes

Pineapple Chicken Rice Bowl

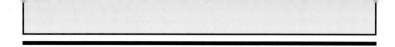

TANDOORI STYLE GRILLED CHICKEN

3½ pounds broiler-fryer chicken
　　serving pieces
1 container (8 ounces) plain
　　lowfat yogurt
1 medium onion, quartered
2 large cloves garlic

2 tablespoons curry power
1 tablespoon paprika
1½ teaspoons salt
⅛ to ¼ teaspoon ground red
　　pepper

Pierce chicken liberally on meaty side with fork tines, then with sharp knife make ½-inch-deep diagonal cuts about 1 inch apart. Place in 12×8×2-inch glass baking dish; set aside. Combine in food processor or electric blender yogurt, onion, garlic, curry powder, paprika, salt and red pepper. Process until smooth. Set aside ¼ cup yogurt mixture; refrigerate.

Pour remaining yogurt mixture over chicken, turning to coat both sides. Marinate 15 minutes or cover and refrigerate up to 24 hours.

To cook over coals, place chicken on rack over medium-hot coals. Grill chicken, turning often and basting with reserved ¼ cup yogurt mixture. Cook chicken through, 35 to 40 minutes.　　　　　　　*Makes 4 servings*

TO BAKE: Preheat oven to 400°F. Place chicken on rack in broiling pan; bake following directions for grilling. Just before serving, brush with 1 tablespoon melted butter.

Favorite recipe from **National Dairy Board**

ROAST CHICKEN WITH SAVORY
CORNBREAD STUFFING

1 package (8 to 12 ounces) corn
　　muffin mix
　　Ingredients for cornbread
1 tablespoon butter or
　　margarine
2 green onions, diagonally
　　sliced
1 medium red pepper, seeded
　　and diced
4 ribs celery, diced, divided
1 teaspoon grated lemon peel
½ teaspoon dried thyme leaves,
　　crushed

½ teaspoon ground sage
1 teaspoon freshly ground
　　pepper, divided
5 cups chicken broth, divided
1 COOKIN' GOOD® Roaster
　　Chicken (6 pounds)
　　Salt
2 medium carrots, thinly sliced
1 medium potato, peeled and
　　diced
1 small onion, thinly sliced
2 cloves garlic
1 bay leaf

Roast Chicken with Savory Cornbread Stuffing

1. Prepare corn muffin mix according to package directions for cornbread. Cool completely. Turn oven control to 350°F.

2. Melt butter in 10-inch skillet over medium heat. Cook green onions, red pepper and half the celery 10 minutes or until tender. Stir in lemon peel, thyme, sage and ½ teaspoon pepper; set aside.

3. Coarsely crumble cornbread into medium bowl. Stir in celery mixture and 1 cup chicken broth.

4. Rinse Roaster with cold water and drain well; pat dry with paper towels. Spoon stuffing into body cavity. Close by folding skin over opening; skewer if necessary. With cotton strings, tie legs and tail together. Sprinkle Roaster with salt and remaining ½ teaspoon pepper.

5. Place chicken into large roasting pan. Add carrots, potato, onion, garlic, bay leaf, remaining 4 cups chicken broth and remaining celery. Insert meat thermometer into thickest part of thigh, being careful pointed end of thermometer does not touch bone. Bake roaster about 2½ hours, checking often during last half hour of roasting. Roaster is done when temperature reaches 180°F or when juices run clear when pierced with fork.

6. Remove Roaster to serving platter; keep warm. Pour broth mixture into large measuring cup or bowl; discard bay leaf. Let stand a few seconds until fat separates from broth. Skim fat; blend mixture in food processor or blender until smooth. Reheat sauce before serving.

Makes 6 servings

CHICKEN WITH SNOW PEAS AND WALNUTS

SAUCE

1 tablespoon butter or
   margarine
1 tablespoon all-purpose flour
2 teaspoons dried basil leaves,
   crushed
1 teaspoon lemon pepper
½ teaspoon salt

½ teaspoon garlic powder
1½ cups (12-ounce can) *undiluted*
   CARNATION® Evaporated
   Milk
¼ cup dry vermouth or chicken
   broth

CHICKEN AND VEGETABLES

2 tablespoons olive oil, divided
1 pound boneless skinless
   chicken breasts, cut into
   strips
1 cup (4½ ounces) *thinly* sliced
   or julienned carrots

2 cups (5 ounces) Chinese snow
   peas, ends removed
1 cup (3 ounces) sliced fresh
   mushrooms
   Cooked rice or pasta (optional)
¼ cup chopped walnuts, toasted

For sauce, in medium saucepan, melt butter; whisk in flour, basil, lemon pepper, salt, garlic powder, and evaporated milk. Stir constantly over medium heat until thickened. Stir in vermouth. Cover; keep warm.

For chicken and vegetables, in large skillet over medium heat, heat *1 tablespoon* oil. Add chicken; cook 5 to 6 minutes, stirring frequently until cooked. Remove and set aside. Add *remaining* 1 tablespoon oil to skillet; stir-fry carrots over high heat for 1 minute. Add snow peas and mushrooms; cook until crisp-tender. Combine chicken pieces with vegetables in skillet. Serve over hot cooked rice, if desired. Pour sauce over top; sprinkle with walnuts.   *Makes 4 servings*

GOLDEN GLAZED CHICKEN BREASTS

1 envelope LIPTON® Recipe
   Secrets™ Onion Recipe
   Soup Mix
⅔ cup apricot preserves or
   peach-apricot sauce
½ cup water

1 pound boneless skinless
   chicken breasts
2 large red or green peppers,
   sliced
   Hot cooked rice

In small bowl, thoroughly combine onion recipe soup mix, apricot preserves and water; set aside.

In foil-lined broiler pan, arrange chicken breasts and peppers; top with soup mixture. Broil 10 minutes or until chicken is tender and done, turning once. Serve over hot rice.   *Makes about 4 servings*

Chicken with Snow Peas and Walnuts

Apple-Stuffed Chicken Breasts

APPLE-STUFFED CHICKEN BREASTS

1 boneless skinless chicken
    breast, halved
½ cup chopped WASHINGTON
    Apple*
2 tablespoons shredded
    Cheddar cheese
1 tablespoon fine dry bread
    crumbs

1 tablespoon butter or
    margarine
¼ cup dry white wine
    Water
1½ teaspoons cornstarch
    Chopped parsley

Pound chicken pieces, between 2 pieces of waxed paper, to ¼-inch thickness with flat side of meat mallet or chef's knife.

Combine apple, cheese and bread crumbs; divide between chicken pieces. Roll up each chicken breast; secure with wooden toothpicks. Melt butter in 7-inch skillet; cook chicken breasts, turning to brown both sides. Add wine and ¼ cup water. Cover; simmer 15 to 20 minutes until chicken is no longer pink. Remove chicken from pan. Remove toothpicks before serving. Combine 1 tablespoon water and cornstarch; stir into juices in pan. Cook and stir until thickened. Pour gravy over breasts; garnish with parsley.

Makes 2 servings

*Golden Delicious, Granny Smith, Newtown Pippin, Rome Beauty and/or Winesap apples may be used.

Favorite recipe from **Washington Apple Commission**

CHICKEN ALMONDINE

6 tablespoons (¾ stick)
   margarine or butter, melted
½ teaspoon garlic powder
3 cups HONEY ALMOND
   DELIGHT® brand cereal,
   crushed to 1½ cups

2 boneless skinless chicken
   breasts, halved (about
   1½ pounds)
1 jar (10 ounces) sweet and sour
   sauce

Preheat oven to 375°F. In shallow dish combine margarine and garlic powder. Pour cereal into large plastic bag. Dip chicken into margarine. Place chicken in bag and shake to coat evenly. Place chicken on rack in shallow baking pan. Bake 45 minutes or until chicken is no longer pink. Warm sweet and sour sauce until heated through. Spoon warmed sauce over chicken.

Makes 4 servings

Variation: For appetizers, pound chicken to ½-inch thickness with flat side of meat mallet or chef's knife. Cut into 2×1-inch pieces. Bake 20 to 25 minutes. *Makes 40 appetizers.*

CHICKEN KIEV

2 boneless skinless chicken
   breasts, halved (about
   1 pound)
⅓ cup BLUE BONNET® Spread
2 tablespoons chopped chives
½ teaspoon salt

Dash ground black pepper
1 egg
1 tablespoon milk
⅔ cup plain bread crumbs
Oil for frying

Pound chicken pieces to about ¼-inch thickness with flat side of meat mallet or chef's knife. Place 1½ tablespoons spread in center of each breast. Sprinkle spread with chives, salt and pepper. Roll each breast and overlap sides so spread mixture is completely enclosed. Set aside.

Beat together egg and milk. Roll chicken in bread crumbs, then in egg mixture and again in bread crumbs to coat well. Refrigerate at least 20 minutes.

Deep fry chicken rolls in 375°F oil until well browned on all sides, about 8 minutes. Drain on paper towels. Serve hot.

Makes 4 servings

ONE DISH MEALS

CITRUS CHICKEN

1 tablespoon vegetable oil
2 boneless skinless chicken
   breasts, halved (about
   1 pound)
1 cup orange juice
4 teaspoons sugar
1 clove garlic, minced

1 teaspoon dried rosemary
   leaves, crushed
2 teaspoons cornstarch
¼ cup dry white wine
   Salt and pepper
2 pink grapefruit, sectioned

Heat oil in large skillet over medium heat; add chicken. Cook about
8 minutes, turning once or until no longer pink in center. Remove chicken
from skillet; keep warm.

Add orange juice, sugar, garlic and rosemary to skillet; bring to a boil.
Combine cornstarch and wine in cup until smooth. Add to skillet; cook,
stirring constantly, until sauce is clear and thickened. Season with salt and
pepper to taste. Add grapefruit; heat through, stirring occasionally. Serve
over chicken. *Makes 4 servings*

CHICKEN, BROCCOLI & RICE SOUP

4½ cups water
  2 cups cubed cooked chicken
  1 package LIPTON® Golden
     Sauté Rice Mix—Chicken &
     Broccoli

1 cup shredded Cheddar
   cheese (about 4 ounces)

In large saucepan, combine all ingredients except cheese; bring to a boil.
Reduce heat and simmer, uncovered, stirring occasionally, 10 minutes. To
serve, evenly pour into 4 bowls, then top each with ¼ cup cheese.
Makes 4 (1½ cup) servings

Citrus Chicken

Artichoke Chicken Pilaf

ARTICHOKE CHICKEN PILAF

2 tablespoons butter or margarine
12 ounces boneless skinless chicken breasts, cut into strips
1 clove garlic, minced
1¾ cups water
1 package (6 ounces) MJB/FARMHOUSE® Rice Pilaf Mix
½ teaspoon basil leaves, crushed
1 jar (6 ounces) marinated artichokes, drained, rinsed and cut into halves
3 green onions, cut into ½-inch lengths
¼ cup toasted sliced almonds

Heat butter in large skillet over medium-high heat. Cook and stir chicken and garlic in butter 5 to 7 minutes or until browned. Add water, seasoning mix, rice and basil. Bring to a boil. Reduce heat to low. Cover and simmer 15 minutes. Stir in artichokes and green onions; cook 5 minutes more. Garnish with almonds. *Makes about 4 servings*

CHICKEN CUTLETS PARMESAN

2 boneless skinless chicken breasts, halved
Salt and pepper to taste
2 tablespoons olive oil
1 jar (14 ounces) spaghetti sauce with mushrooms
¼ cup sliced pitted ripe olives
2 tablespoons grated Parmesan cheese
Hot cooked spaghetti

Pound chicken breasts to ½-inch thickness with flat side of meat mallet or chef's knife. Sprinkle salt and pepper over chicken. Heat oil in large skillet over medium-high heat. Add chicken and cook, turning to brown on both sides, about 8 minutes. Drain off excess fat.

Spoon spaghetti sauce over chicken; top with olives. Cook over medium heat about 5 minutes or until chicken is fork-tender and sauce is bubbly. Sprinkle cheese over all. Cover; let stand 2 minutes or until cheese melts. Serve with cooked spaghetti.   *Makes 4 servings*

Favorite recipe from **Delmarva Poultry Industry, Inc.**

HEARTY LANCASTER CHICKEN, VEGETABLE AND DUMPLING SOUP

6 cups chicken stock or broth
**2 cups diced cooked PERDUE®
    Chicken**
**1 package (10 ounces) frozen
    corn *or* kernels from 2 ears
    fresh corn**
**1 cup thinly sliced leek, white
    and tender green parts only
    or 1 medium onion, thinly
    sliced**

**½ cup parboiled potatoes, cut
    into ½-inch cubes**
**½ cup parboiled carrots, cut into
    ½-inch pieces**
½ cup shredded green cabbage
1 teaspoon salt
**⅛ teaspoon freshly ground
    pepper**
Knepp (recipe follows)

Heat broth to boiling in large saucepan over high heat. Add all remaining ingredients except Knepp. Reduce heat to low. Cover and simmer 3 minutes while making dumplings.

Drop dumpling batter by half teaspoons into simmering soup. Stir in parsley when dumplings rise to top; serve.   *Makes 4 servings*

KNEPP (LITTLE DUMPLINGS)

1 egg
¾ cup all-purpose flour
⅓ cup water
¼ teaspoon salt

⅛ teaspoon baking powder
Pinch ground nutmeg
**1 teaspoon chopped fresh
    parsley (optional)**

Beat egg in small bowl; stir in flour, water, salt, baking powder, nutmeg and parsley.

Chicken Spinach Stracciatella: Omit dumplings. Clean and stem ½ pound fresh spinach; stack and cut into ½-inch strips. Whisk together 2 eggs with ½ cup grated Parmesan cheese. Stir in spinach with chicken, then heat soup to boiling. Stir soup constantly while pouring in egg mixture in thin stream. Cook until soup simmers again; stir gently just before serving.

CREAMY HERBED CHICKEN

1 package (9 ounces) fresh
    bow-tie pasta or fusilli*
1 tablespoon vegetable oil
2 boneless skinless chicken
    breasts, halved (about
    1 pound) cut into ½-inch
    strips
1 small red onion, cut into slices

1 package (10 ounces) frozen
    green peas, thawed, drained
1 yellow or red pepper, cut into
    strips
½ cup chicken broth
1 container (8 ounces) soft
    cream cheese with garlic
    and herbs
Salt and black pepper

Cook pasta in lightly salted boiling water according to package directions, about 5 minutes; drain.

Meanwhile, heat oil in large skillet or wok over medium-high heat. Add chicken and onion; stir-fry 3 minutes or until chicken is no longer pink in center. Add peas and yellow pepper; stir-fry 4 minutes. Reduce heat to medium.

Stir in broth and cream cheese. Cook, stirring constantly, until cream cheese is melted. Combine pasta and chicken mixture in serving bowl; mix lightly. Season with salt and black pepper to taste. Garnish as desired.
Makes 4 servings

*Substitute dried bow-tie pasta or fusilli for fresh pasta. Cooking time will be longer; follow package directions.

NO-PEEK CHICKEN AND RICE

2 tablespoons vegetable oil
1 broiler-fryer chicken, cut into
    serving pieces (2½ to
    3 pounds)
2½ cups water

1 envelope LIPTON® Recipe
    Secrets™ Vegetable Recipe
    Soup Mix
½ teaspoon dried basil leaves,
    crushed
¾ cup uncooked regular rice

In large skillet, heat oil over medium heat and add chicken, browning 2 minutes on each side; drain. Stir in water, vegetable recipe soup mix and basil. Bring to a boil, then stir in uncooked rice. Simmer, covered, 45 minutes or until chicken and rice are done.
Makes about 4 servings

Creamy Herbed Chicken

CHICKEN AND SHRIMP GUMBO

1 can (8¾ ounces) DEL
   MONTE® Whole Kernel
   Golden Sweet Corn
1 can (8½ ounces) DEL
   MONTE® Green Lima Beans
1 can (14½ ounces) DEL
   MONTE® Original Stewed
   Tomatoes (No Salt Added)
1 boneless skinless chicken
   breast, cut into cubes
1 cup sliced fresh or frozen okra
1 cup green pepper strips
2 cloves garlic, minced
¼ teaspoon *each* allspice,
   ground red pepper, black
   pepper
6 ounces medium shrimp,
   shelled, deveined
3 cups hot cooked brown rice

Drain corn and beans reserving liquid; pour liquid into large heavy pot or saucepan. Add tomatoes, chicken, okra, green pepper, garlic and seasonings. Bring to a boil. Reduce heat to medium and cook 6 to 8 minutes until thickened. Stir in corn and beans; heat through. Just before serving, stir in shrimp and cook until shrimp are opaque. Serve over rice.

Makes 4 servings

Prep time: 10 minutes   **Cook time:** 20 minutes

SAUCY CHICKEN AND RICE SKILLET

2 tablespoons butter or
   margarine
¾ pound boneless skinless
   chicken breasts, cut into
   ½-inch cubes
1 cup chopped tomatoes
½ cup chopped onion
1 clove garlic, minced
½ teaspoon dried basil leaves,
   crushed
¼ teaspoon dried oregano
   leaves, crushed
1½ cups water
¼ cup dry white wine
1 package (6 ounces) MJB/
   FARMHOUSE® Chicken
   Brown Rice
3 tablespoons grated Parmesan
   cheese

Heat butter in large skillet over medium-high heat. Cook and stir chicken, tomatoes, onion, garlic, basil and oregano in butter 5 to 7 minutes or until chicken is no longer pink. Add water and wine. Bring to a boil over high heat. Add rice and seasoning mix; reduce heat to low. Cover and simmer 20 to 25 minutes or until water is absorbed. Stir in Parmesan cheese.

Makes 4 servings

CHICKEN BREASTS SEVILLE

2 tablespoons butter or margarine
4 boneless skinless chicken breasts, halved
2 cans (16 ounces *each*) whole potatoes, drained
1 teaspoon dried thyme leaves, crushed
1 teaspoon dried tarragon leaves, crushed
1 teaspoon dried savory leaves, crushed
2 cans (8 ounces *each*) whole baby onions, drained

1 can (15 ounces) pitted ripe olives, drained
1 jar (15 ounces) roasted sweet red peppers, drained, cut into large pieces
1 can (14 ounces) artichoke hearts or bottoms, drained
1 can (13¾ ounces) chicken broth
½ cup dry vermouth
¼ cup Dijon-style mustard
2 tablespoons cold water
1 tablespoon cornstarch
Black pepper
Minced parsley

Heat butter in large skillet over medium-high heat. Cook chicken breasts until browned on both sides, about 10 minutes. Add potatoes, thyme, tarragon and savory; cook over medium heat 5 minutes. Add onions, olives, red peppers, artichoke hearts, broth, vermouth and mustard. Bring to a boil over high heat. Reduce heat to low. Cover and simmer until chicken is no longer pink in center, about 10 minutes.

Mix water and cornstarch in small mixing bowl; stir into skillet. Cook over high heat 1 to 2 minutes until thickened. Season with black pepper. Arrange chicken and vegetables on deep platter; sprinkle with parsley.

Makes 8 servings

Favorite recipe from **Canned Food Information Council**

CREAMED CHICKEN

1 can (12 fluid ounces) PET® Evaporated Milk
2 teaspoons flour
1 green or red bell pepper, chopped

1 teaspoon chicken bouillon granules *or* 1 cube chicken bouillon
¼ teaspoon ground black pepper
1½ cups cubed cooked chicken
Toast points *or* patty shells

In medium saucepan, mix evaporated milk and flour until well blended; add green pepper, bouillon and ground pepper. Heat over medium heat, stirring constantly, until mixture boils and thickens. Add chicken and continue cooking until chicken is heated. Serve on toast points or in patty shells.

Makes 4 (½ cup) servings

CHICKEN WITH SHERRY SAUCE

3 boneless skinless chicken
    breasts, halved (about
    1¾ pounds)
⅛ teaspoon salt
⅛ teaspoon pepper
2 tablespoons margarine or
    butter
½ cup dry sherry

1 can (4 ounces) button
    mushrooms, undrained
Undiluted CARNATION®
    Evaporated Milk
1 package (.87 ounce) chicken
    gravy mix
1 cup (8 ounces) sour cream

Lightly sprinkle chicken breasts with salt and pepper. In 10 or 12-inch skillet over medium-high heat, melt margarine; brown chicken on both sides. Add sherry, mushrooms, and mushroom liquid. Reduce heat; cover and cook for 20 to 25 minutes or until chicken is cooked through.

With slotted spoon, remove chicken and mushrooms to serving dish; cover and keep warm. Measure pan juices; if necessary, add evaporated milk to make 1¼ cups liquid. In same skillet, combine liquid and chicken gravy mix. Bring to a boil; reduce heat and simmer uncovered for 5 minutes, stirring constantly. Cool slightly. Stir in ½ cup undiluted evaporated milk and sour cream; heat gently, stirring until warmed through. Do not boil. Pour over chicken. *Makes 6 servings*

CHICKEN THIGHS AND VEGETABLES LYONNAISE

2 medium-size baking potatoes,
    peeled and thinly sliced
    (about 2 cups)
1 package (2 pounds) PERDUE®
    Chicken Thighs (6 thighs)
½ teaspoon ground thyme,
    divided
Salt to taste
Ground pepper to taste

4 medium-size carrots, peeled
    and thinly sliced (about
    2 cups)
1 medium-size onion, peeled
    and thinly sliced (about
    1 cup)
4 teaspoons butter or margarine
1 cup milk or heavy cream
¼ teaspoon hot pepper sauce
    Paprika

Soak sliced potatoes in large bowl in cold water for at least 10 minutes. Preheat oven to 350°F. Sprinkle thighs with ¼ teaspoon thyme, salt and pepper. Drain potatoes well in a colander. Layer with carrots and onion in buttered 11×8-inch baking dish. Season each layer with remaining ¼ teaspoon thyme, salt and pepper. Dot lightly with butter. Arrange chicken, skin side up, on top of vegetables. Combine milk and hot pepper sauce and pour over chicken; sprinkle generously with paprika.

Bake 60 to 70 minutes until chicken and vegetables are tender.
Makes 4 servings

Quick Arroz con Pollo

QUICK ARROZ CON POLLO

2 tablespoons olive or
    vegetable oil
¾ pound boneless chicken
    breasts, cut into 1-inch
    cubes
½ cup chopped onion
1 clove garlic, minced
1¾ cups water

1 medium tomato, chopped
1 package (6 ounces) MJB/
    FARMHOUSE® Savory
    Chicken Rice Mix
⅓ cup frozen peas, thawed
⅓ cup sliced pimento-stuffed
    green olives or sliced pitted
    ripe olives

Heat oil in large skillet over medium-high heat. Cook and stir chicken, onion
and garlic in oil 5 to 7 minutes or until chicken is no longer pink. Add water
and tomato. Bring to a boil over high heat. Add rice and seasoning mix.
Reduce heat to low. Cover and simmer 15 minutes. Add peas and olives;
cook 5 to 10 minutes longer or until liquid is absorbed.

Makes 4 to 6 servings

SWEET 'N SOUR CHICKEN

1 can (20 ounces) DOLE®
  Pineapple Chunks in Juice
2 boneless skinless chicken
  breasts
  Salt and pepper to taste
1 teaspoon vegetable oil
2 DOLE® Carrots, thinly sliced
1 DOLE® Green Bell Pepper,
  seeded, chunked
1 medium onion, chunked

1 clove garlic, pressed
½ cup catsup
⅓ cup light brown sugar, packed
1 tablespoon cornstarch
1 tablespoon soy sauce
1 teaspoon ground ginger
  Grated peel and juice from
  1 DOLE® Lemon
2 cups hot cooked rice

• Drain pineapple; reserve juice.

• Cut chicken into bite-size pieces. Season with salt and pepper.

• In large nonstick skillet heat oil over medium-high heat; brown chicken,
  turning once. Reduce heat. Add carrots, bell pepper, onion and garlic to
  skillet. Cover; simmer 5 minutes.

• Combine reserved juice, catsup, brown sugar, constarch, soy sauce,
  ginger, lemon peel and lemon juice in small bowl until blended. Stir into
  same skillet. Cover; simmer 10 minutes longer. Stir in pineapple; heat
  through. Serve with rice.   *Makes 4 servings*

Prep time: 15 minutes   **Cook time:** 15 minutes

NEW ENGLAND CHICKEN 'N' CORN CHOWDER

¼ pound bacon or salt pork,
  diced
1 cup chopped onion
½ cup chopped celery
4 cups chicken stock or broth
2 cups, ½-inch cubed, peeled
  potatoes
1 package (10 ounces) frozen
  corn

1 teaspoon salt
⅛ teaspoon freshly ground
  pepper
2 cups diced cooked PERDUE®
  Chicken
1 cup (½ pint) heavy cream
  Oyster crackers (optional)

Cook and stir bacon in large saucepan over medium-high heat, 3 minutes,
until bacon is light brown. Add onion and celery; cook 3 minutes longer. Stir
in stock. Bring to a boil over high heat. Add potatoes, corn, salt and pepper;
cook 5 to 10 minutes until potatoes are tender. Stir in chicken and cream.
Reduce heat to low. Cover and simmer 3 minutes. Serve with oyster
crackers.   *Makes 4 to 6 servings*

Sweet 'n Sour Chicken

CHICKEN SAUCE PIQUANT

4 tablespoons Chef Paul
    Prudhomme's® POULTRY
    MAGIC®
1 cup all-purpose flour
2 broiler-fryer chickens, each
    cut into 8 pieces (2½ to
    3 pounds *each*)
    Vegetable oil for frying
1¾ cups chopped onions
1¾ cups chopped celery
1¾ cups chopped green bell
    peppers

1¾ cups peeled and chopped
    tomatoes
3 tablespoons finely chopped
    jalapeño peppers*
2 tablespoons minced garlic
1¾ cups canned tomato sauce
1 tablespoon plus 2 teaspoons
    hot pepper sauce
4 cups chicken stock
    Hot cooked rice (preferably
    converted)

In paper or plastic bag, mix 1 tablespoon Poultry Magic® into flour. Remove and discard excess fat from chicken pieces; sprinkle chicken evenly with remaining Poultry Magic®. Coat chicken in seasoned flour.

In large skillet heat ½ inch oil to 350°F. Fry chicken, skin-side down, (large pieces first) until browned and crispy on both sides and meat is cooked, about 5 to 8 minutes per side. Do not crowd. (Maintain temperature as close to 350°F as possible; turn heat down if drippings start getting dark red-brown. Do not let drippings burn.) Drain on paper towels.

Carefully pour hot oil from skillet into glass measuring cup, leaving as many brown bits in pan as possible. Return ¼ cup hot oil to skillet. Turn heat to high. Using spoon, loosen any brown bits stuck to pan bottom. Stir in onions, celery and bell peppers; cook, stirring constantly, scraping pan bottom well, until brown bits are mixed into vegetables. Add tomatoes, jalapeño peppers and garlic; stir well. Cook about 2 minutes, stirring once or twice. Add tomato sauce; cook, stirring occasionally, about 3 minutes. Stir in hot pepper sauce; remove from heat.

Heat serving plates in 250°F oven. Meanwhile, place chicken pieces and stock in 5½-quart saucepan or large Dutch oven. Bring to a boil over medium-high heat. Reduce heat to medium. Cover and cook 5 minutes. Stir half the tomato mixture into stock. Reduce heat to low. Cover and simmer 5 minutes. Stir in remaining tomato mixture. Cover; simmer, stirring occasionally, 8 to 10 minutes more. Remove from heat; serve immediately over rice. *Makes 8 servings*

*Fresh jalapeños are preferred; if you have to use pickled ones, rinse as much vinegar from them as possible.

Golden Apple Mulligatawny

GOLDEN APPLE MULLIGATAWNY

2 tablespoons vegetable oil
1 broiler-fryer chicken, cut into serving pieces (2½ pounds)
6 cups water
1 teaspoon salt, divided
2 tablespoons butter or margarine
2 WASHINGTON Golden Delicious apples, cored and chopped
1 small onion, chopped

1 small sweet red pepper, chopped
½ cup chopped carrots
½ cup chopped celery
1½ teaspoons curry powder
1 tablespoon all-purpose flour
¼ teaspoon ground black pepper
⅛ teaspoon ground cloves
⅛ teaspoon ground red pepper
2 cups cooked rice
¼ cup chopped fresh parsley leaves

1. Heat oil in Dutch oven over medium-high heat. Add chicken; cook until brown on all sides. Drain excess fat. Add water and ½ teaspoon salt. Reduce heat to low. Cover and simmer 1 hour.

2. Remove chicken from liquid; set aside to cool slightly. Reserve liquid in separate container. Cool chicken; remove skin and bones and discard. Cut remaining chicken into bite-size pieces; set aside.

3. Melt butter in same Dutch oven; add apples, onion, red pepper, carrots and celery. Cook and stir over medium-high heat until apples are just tender. Add curry powder; cook and stir 2 minutes. Blend in flour, black pepper, cloves and ground red pepper. Stir reserved liquid into apple mixture. Reduce heat to low. Cover and simmer 15 minutes.

4. Just before serving, add reserved chicken and remaining ½ teaspoon salt; heat through. To serve, place ⅓ cup rice in each soup bowl; ladle soup over rice. Sprinkle with parsley and serve. *Makes 6 servings*

Favorite recipe from **Washington Apple Commission**

SPICY FRUITED CHICKEN

1 medium DOLE® Fresh Pineapple
2 teaspoons margarine, divided
2 boneless skinless chicken breasts, halved
1 teaspoon garlic powder
Salt to taste
½ large DOLE® Red Bell Pepper, cut into strips
1 cup *each* chunked green and red onion
1 teaspoon minced serrano or jalapeño chile

1 head DOLE® Cabbage, cut into 8 wedges
⅔ cup chicken broth
Grated peel and juice from 1 DOLE® Orange
¼ cup chutney, chopped
1 tablespoon red wine vinegar
½ teaspoon *each* ground cumin, allspice
1½ teaspoons *each* cornstarch, water

• Twist crown from pineapple. Cut pineapple in half lengthwise. Refrigerate half for another use. Cut fruit from shell; cut crosswise into slices. In nonstick skillet heat 1 teaspoon margarine over medium-high heat; brown pineapple, turning once. Remove to plate.

• Pound chicken breasts lightly until even thickness with flat side of meat mallet or chef's knife. Sprinkle with garlic powder and salt. Heat remaining 1 teaspoon margarine over medium-high heat; brown chicken, turning once. Reduce heat. Cover; cook 10 minutes. Remove to plate.

• Cook and stir bell pepper, onions and chile in pan drippings 2 minutes. Arrange cabbage in skillet. Add chicken broth, orange peel, ⅓ cup orange juice, chutney, vinegar, cumin and allspice. Bring to a boil. Reduce heat. Cover; simmer 6 minutes. Remove cabbage with slotted spoon to platter. Blend cornstarch and water in skillet. Cook, stirring, until sauce boils and thickens.

• Slice chicken; serve with cabbage, pineapple and sauce.

Makes 4 servings

Prep time: 25 minutes   **Cook time:** 30 minutes

Spicy Fruited Chicken

Chicken to the Macs

CHICKEN TO THE MACS

1 (7-ounce) package CREAMETTES® Elbow Macaroni (2 cups uncooked)	2 cups milk
	1 (10¾-ounce) can cream of mushroom soup
2 cups broccoli flowerets	1 teaspoon salt
¼ cup margarine or butter	¼ teaspoon black pepper
1 small red bell pepper, sliced	2 cups (8 ounces) shredded Cheddar cheese, divided
1 small onion, chopped	
1 cup sliced fresh mushrooms	2 cups cubed cooked chicken

Prepare Creamettes® Elbow Macaroni according to package directions, adding broccoli the last 4 minutes of cooking time; drain. In large skillet heat margarine; add red pepper, onion and mushrooms and cook until onion is tender. Add milk, soup, salt and black pepper. Cook and stir for 5 minutes. Stir in 1 cup cheese and chicken. Combine macaroni and broccoli with soup mixture. Pour into a 2½-quart baking dish; top with remaining cheese. Cover; bake in 350°F oven 20 to 30 minutes, until hot and bubbly. Refrigerate leftovers.

Makes 4 to 6 servings

BRUNSWICK STEW

1 broiler-fryer chicken, cut into 8 serving pieces (2½ to 3 pounds)
1 (13¾-fluid-ounce) can COLLEGE INN® Chicken Broth
2 (6-ounce) cans tomato paste
2 tablespoons REGINA® Red Wine Vinegar
2 tablespoons Worcestershire sauce
¼ teaspoon ground red pepper
2 cups cubed cooked pork
1 (17-ounce) can lima beans, undrained
1 (16-ounce) can peeled tomatoes, undrained and coarsely chopped

In large heavy saucepan, over medium-high heat, heat chicken, broth, tomato paste, vinegar, Worcestershire sauce and red pepper to a boil. Cover; reduce heat and simmer 20 minutes. Add pork, lima beans and tomatoes. Cover; simmer 20 to 25 minutes longer or until chicken is done.

Makes 6 servings

MICROWAVE DIRECTIONS: In 5-quart microwavable casserole, combine first 6 ingredients as above. Cover with waxed paper. Microwave on MEDIUM (50% power) for 28 to 30 minutes, stirring twice during cooking time. Add pork, lima beans and tomatoes; cover. Microwave on LOW (30% power) for 18 to 20 minutes or until chicken is done. Let stand, covered, 10 minutes before serving.

PINEAPPLE CHICKEN PACKETS

1 can (8 ounces) DOLE® Pineapple Slices in Juice
1 cup slivered DOLE® Carrots
1 boneless skinless chicken breast, quartered lengthwise
Salt and pepper to taste
½ teaspoon dried tarragon leaves, crushed
Grated peel and juice from 1 DOLE® Lemon
1 DOLE® Green Onion, thinly sliced

• Drain pineapple; reserve juice for another use.

• For each packet, arrange ½ cup carrots in center of 12-inch square heavy aluminum foil. Layer 2 pineapple slices, 2 pieces chicken, salt, pepper, tarragon, ½ teaspoon lemon peel, 1 teaspoon lemon juice and ½ onion on each. Fold foil to form packet.

• Place packets on baking sheet. Bake in 450°F oven 15 minutes. Remove from oven. Let stand 5 minutes.

Makes 2 servings

Prep time: 20 minutes   **Cook time:** 15 minutes

INTERNATIONAL ENTRÉES

CHICKEN AND VEGETABLE COUSCOUS

**3 boneless skinless chicken
  breasts (3 ounces *each*)**
1 tablespoon vegetable oil
½ cup chopped green onions
3 garlic cloves, minced
1¼ cups tomato sauce
¼ cup water
1¼ cups chopped carrots
**1 cup canned small white
  beans, drained and rinsed**
1 large potato, cut into cubes

1 yellow squash, chopped
1 medium tomato, chopped
**¼ cup chopped seeded red
  pepper**
¼ cup raisins
2 tablespoons brown sugar
2 teaspoons ground cumin
¾ teaspoon ground cinnamon
3 to 4 drops hot pepper sauce
1½ cups water
1 cup dry couscous

Cut chicken into 3-inch cubes; set aside. Heat oil in skillet over medium heat. Add chicken and cook, turning to brown on all sides. Add green onions and garlic; cook and stir 1 minute. Stir in tomato sauce and ¼ cup water. Add remaining ingredients except 1½ cups water and couscous. Reduce heat to low. Cover and simmer 15 minutes. Meanwhile bring remaining 1½ cups water to a boil over high heat; add couscous. Cover; remove from heat. Let stand 5 minutes. Serve chicken and vegetables over couscous.

Makes 6 servings

Favorite recipe from **The Sugar Association, Inc.**

Chicken and Vegetable Couscous

Surprisingly Simple Chicken Cacciatore

SURPRISINGLY SIMPLE CHICKEN CACCIATORE

4 boneless skinless chicken
   breasts (4 ounces *each*),
   chunked
Salt and pepper
Flour
Paprika
4 tablespoons olive oil, divided
2 cloves garlic, minced
1 (26-ounce) jar CLASSICO®
   Di Napoli Tomato and Basil
   Pasta Sauce

1 small green bell pepper, cut
   into thin strips
1 small red bell pepper, cut into
   thin strips
½ of a (1-pound) package
   CREAMETTE® Thin
   Spaghetti, uncooked
1 cup (4 ounces) shredded
   Provolone cheese

Season chicken with salt and pepper, then coat with flour and sprinkle with paprika. In large skillet, heat 3 tablespoons oil. Brown chicken and garlic; drain. Stir in Classico® Pasta Sauce. Bring to a boil; reduce heat. Cover; simmer 20 minutes, adding green and red bell peppers last 5 minutes. Prepare Creamette® Thin Spaghetti according to package directions; drain and toss with remaining 1 tablespoon oil. Arrange on warm serving platter; top with hot chicken, sauce and cheese. Serve immediately. Refrigerate leftovers. *Makes 4 servings*

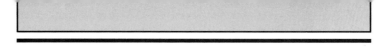

NEW YEAR CHICKEN

¾ cup (3 ounces) shredded
Cheddar cheese
4 strips bacon, cooked and
finely crumbled
2 tablespoons finely chopped
onion
1 teaspoon hot pepper sauce
2 boneless skinless chicken
breasts, halved

2 tablespoons all-purpose flour
½ teaspoon seasoned salt
1 egg, beaten
2 cups Corn CHEX® brand
cereal, crushed to ¾ cup
1 teaspoon dried thyme leaves,
crushed

Preheat oven to 350°F. In small bowl combine cheese, bacon, onion and
pepper sauce. Pound chicken breasts flat to ¼-inch thickness with flat side
of meat mallet or chef's knife. Spread ¼ cup cheese mixture onto each
chicken breast. Roll up chicken breasts securing all ends with wooden picks.

In shallow bowl combine flour and seasoned salt. In separate shallow bowl
place egg. In third shallow bowl combine cereal and thyme. Dip each
chicken breast first into flour mixture, then egg and then cereal mixture.
Place in ungreased 9-inch square baking pan. Bake 35 to 40 minutes or until
chicken is no longer pink. Remove toothpicks before serving.

Makes 4 servings

CHICKEN CORDON DOUX®

3 boneless skinless chicken
breasts, halved
6 slices DOUX DE MONTAGNE®
cheese
6 paper-thin slices prosciutto or
ham
Dry mustard
1½ cups fine, dry bread crumbs
½ teaspoon salt

½ teaspoon pepper
½ teaspoon mixed herbs (sage,
parsley, thyme, rosemary,
bay leaves)
2 eggs, lightly beaten
¼ cup olive oil
¼ cup butter
1 cup dry white wine
Cooked brown rice

Pound chicken breasts until paper thin, between 2 pieces of waxed paper,
with flat side of meat mallet or chef's knife. Place slice of cheese and slice of
ham on each piece of chicken; sprinkle with a little dry mustard. Roll up and
fasten with wooden toothpicks.

Combine bread crumbs, salt, pepper and herb mixture. Dip each roll into
eggs and then into bread crumb mixture. Refrigerate until ready to use (up
to 8 hours). Heat oil and butter in skillet. Brown chicken rolls 10 to
12 minutes on each side; remove from pan. Remove toothpicks before
serving. Add wine to pan; simmer, stirring in all brown bits from bottom and
sides. Pour sauce over chicken rolls. Serve with brown rice.

Makes 6 servings

COLD LIME CHICKEN AND COUSCOUS

¼ cup olive oil, divided
1 medium onion, chopped
  (½ cup)
1¾ cups chicken broth, divided
1 cup couscous
⅓ cup fresh lime juice, divided
2 small cloves garlic, pressed,
  divided
1 teaspoon grated lime peel,
  divided
¾ teaspoon salt, divided

¼ teaspoon freshly ground black
  pepper, divided
5 green onions, trimmed, cut on
  diagonal into 1-inch pieces
1 small green bell pepper, cut
  into ½-inch pieces
1 small red bell pepper, cut into
  ½-inch pieces
4 COOKIN' GOOD® Whole
  Broiler or Roaster Chicken
  Legs or 4 Thighs and
  4 Drumsticks
Leaf lettuce greens

Heat 1 tablespoon oil in 10-inch heavy skillet over medium-high heat. Add onion; cook, stirring occasionally about 5 minutes, or until onion is tender. Add 1½ cups broth, couscous, 3 tablespoons lime juice, 1 clove garlic, ½ teaspoon lime peel, ¼ teaspoon salt and ⅛ teaspoon pepper. Bring to a boil over medium-high heat; cook about 2 minutes. Remove skillet from heat; cover and let stand 5 minutes. Remove lid; transfer mixture to large bowl. Cover; refrigerate for several hours.

Meanwhile, heat 1 tablespoon remaining oil in same skillet over medium heat. Add green onions, green and red peppers; cook, stirring occasionally about 2 minutes, or until vegetables are just tender. Add cooked onions and peppers along with remaining ½ teaspoon grated lime peel to mixture in refrigerator.

Heat remaining 2 tablespoons oil in skillet over medium-high heat. Sprinkle chicken with remaining ½ teaspoon salt and ⅛ teaspoon pepper and add to skillet. Cook 5 to 7 minutes on each side until golden. Add remaining ¼ cup chicken broth, lime juice and garlic clove; bring to a boil. Reduce heat to low. Simmer 15 to 20 minutes for broiler legs, thighs and drumsticks and 20 to 25 minutes for roaster legs, thighs and drumsticks, or until chicken is tender when pierced with a fork.

To serve, spoon couscous mixture onto lettuce-lined platter. Arrange chicken over couscous mixture. *Makes 4 servings*

Italian Vegetable Chicken

ITALIAN VEGETABLE CHICKEN

1 pound boneless skinless
   chicken breasts, halved
2 cloves garlic, pressed
2 teaspoons Italian herb
   seasoning
   Salt and pepper to taste
1 egg white
½ cup all-purpose flour, divided

1 pound Italian sausage, cut
   into 1-inch chunks
2 teaspoons olive oil (optional)
2 cups sliced mushrooms
1 large onion, chopped
1 DOLE® Red Bell Pepper,
   slivered
1 cup water
2 cups DOLE® Broccoli florettes

• Pound chicken to ¼-inch thickness with flat side of meat mallet or chef's knife. Rub chicken with garlic; sprinkle with herbs, salt and pepper. Dip into egg white; coat with flour.

• In large skillet over medium-high heat, brown sausage. Remove and drain; set aside.

• Add chicken to same skillet, turning to brown both sides. Remove to platter. Add sausage to chicken. Keep warm.

• Add olive oil to skillet if needed. Add mushrooms, onion and red pepper; cook and stir until onion is soft. Add any remaining flour or 1 additional teaspoon flour to skillet. Stir to blend. Continue cooking to brown slightly. Stir in water. Cook and stir until slightly thickened, 3 to 5 minutes. Add broccoli; heat through until crisp-tender. Spoon over chicken.

Makes 6 servings

Prep time: 20 minutes   **Cook time:** 15 minutes

FIESTA CHICKEN SANDWICHES

1 pound COOKIN' GOOD®
  Chicken Tenders
Water
½ teaspoon salt
1½ tablespoons olive oil
  2 tablespoons finely chopped
    onion
¼ cup molasses
  2 tablespoons catsup
1½ tablespoons prepared
    mustard

1½ tablespoons white vinegar
  8 flour tortillas* (6 to 7 inches
    each)
  1 carrot, shredded
  1 small green pepper, halved,
    cored, seeded and finely
    chopped
  1 cup shredded lettuce
  1 medium tomato, chopped
  1 cup (4 ounces) shredded
    Monterey Jack cheese

1. Preheat oven to 325°F.

2. Place chicken in 10-inch skillet. Add water to cover and salt. Bring to a boil over high heat. Reduce heat to low; cover and simmer 10 to 15 minutes, or until chicken is tender and juices run clear when pierced with a fork. Remove to warm platter and cut into 2¼×1-inch strips when cool enough to handle.

3. For barbecue sauce, heat oil in small saucepan over medium heat. Add onion; cook, stirring occasionally, 3 to 5 minutes. Add molasses, catsup, mustard and vinegar; heat to boiling. Reduce heat to low and simmer 10 minutes.

4. Meanwhile, wrap tortillas securely in foil. Warm in preheated oven 5 to 10 minutes.

5. Drain chicken tenders and add to barbecue sauce. Toss together until well-coated and heated through.

6. To assemble sandwiches, place small portion of chicken across center of 1 tortilla. Keep remaining tortillas wrapped in foil. Top with about 1 tablespoon *each* carrot, green pepper, lettuce, tomato and cheese. Fold in sides and secure with wooden pick. Repeat with remaining ingredients to make 7 more sandwiches. Remove toothpicks before serving.

Makes 4 to 6 servings

*Corn tortillas may be substituted for flour tortillas; however, flour tortillas seem more readily available in larger sizes than corn tortillas. Larger-size tortillas are easier to fill and they hold together better.

Fiesta Chicken Sandwiches

SZECHUAN CHICKEN

2 tablespoons reduced-sodium
   soy sauce, divided
1 tablespoon cornstarch
1 pound boneless skinless
   chicken breasts, cut into
   1-inch pieces
1 tablespoon dry sherry
½ to 1 teaspoon crushed red
   pepper

2 tablespoons
   FLEISCHMANN'S®
   Margarine
1 large red pepper, diced
⅓ cup sliced green onions
1 teaspoon grated ginger root
2 cups cooked regular long-
   grain rice, prepared in
   unsalted water

In small bowl, combine 1 tablespoon soy sauce and cornstarch; add chicken, tossing to coat well. Blend remaining 1 tablespoon soy sauce and sherry; set aside.

In large skillet, over medium-high heat, cook crushed red pepper in margarine until pepper turns black. Add chicken mixture; stir-fry for 3 minutes or until no longer pink. Remove chicken from skillet; set aside. In same skillet, stir-fry red pepper, green onions and ginger root for 2 minutes or until tender-crisp. Return chicken to skillet with sherry mixture; cook 2 to 3 minutes more, stirring constantly until chicken is cooked. Serve over rice.

Makes 4 servings

CHICKEN ENCHILADA CASSEROLE

4 uncooked corn tortillas
4 cups cubed, cooked chicken
1 cup KELLOGG'S® ALL-BRAN®
   cereal
1 cup (4 ounces) shredded
   mozzarella cheese
1 jar (10 ounces) enchilada
   sauce

1 can (8 ounces) tomato sauce
1 cup (8 ounces) plain, nonfat
   yogurt
4 cups shredded lettuce
½ cup chopped tomato
⅓ cup sliced green onions

1. Place tortillas on baking sheet. Bake at 350°F about 10 minutes or until crisp. Cool; break into small pieces. Set aside.

2. Combine chicken, Kellogg's® All-Bran® cereal, cheese and sauces. Pour into 1½-quart casserole dish.

3. Bake at 350°F about 30 minutes or until heated through. Remove from oven.

4. Layer yogurt, lettuce, tomato and green onions on top of casserole. Sprinkle with tortilla pieces and serve immediately.   *Makes 6 servings*

Paella

PAELLA

2 tablespoons olive or
    vegetable oil
½ pound boneless skinless
    chicken breasts, cut into
    ½-inch cubes
1 cup chopped onion
¾ cup chopped green bell
    pepper
½ cup smoked ham cubes,
    ¼ inch each
1 clove garlic, minced
1 cup MJB/FARMHOUSE®
    Original Long Grain White
    Rice

1 can (14½ ounces) whole
    peeled tomatoes,
    undrained, broken up
1½ cups water
2 tablespoons dry white wine
2 chicken bouillon cubes
¾ teaspoon dried leaf oregano,
    crushed
⅛ teaspoon ground black pepper
⅛ teaspoon ground turmeric
½ pound uncooked medium
    shrimp, shelled, deveined
½ cup frozen peas, thawed

Heat oil in large skillet over medium-high heat. Add chicken, onion, bell pepper, ham and garlic. Cook 5 to 7 minutes or until chicken is no longer pink. Add rice; stir to coat. Add tomatoes, water, wine, bouillon cubes, oregano, pepper and turmeric. Bring to a boil. Reduce heat to low. Cover; simmer 15 minutes. Add shrimp and peas. Cover; cook 10 minutes longer or until shrimp are opaque and liquid is absorbed. *Makes 4 to 6 servings*

West Indies Curried Drumsticks

WEST INDIES CURRIED DRUMSTICKS

12 broiler-fryer chicken drumsticks
¾ teaspoon salt, divided
½ teaspoon paprika
1 tablespoon cornstarch
1 tablespoon sugar

1 cup orange juice
2 cloves garlic, crushed
1½ teaspoons curry powder
1 teaspoon grated orange peel
½ teaspoon ground ginger
½ cup chopped cashews

Place chicken in large baking dish; sprinkle with ½ teaspoon salt and paprika. Bake in 375°F oven 30 minutes. Mix cornstarch and sugar in small saucepan. Stir in orange juice, garlic, curry powder, orange peel, ginger and remaining ¼ teaspoon salt. Cook and stir over medium heat until mixture boils and thickens. Pour sauce over chicken; bake, basting once with pan juices, about 25 minutes more or until chicken is fork-tender. Sprinkle cashews over chicken. *Makes 6 servings*

Favorite recipe from **Delmarva Poultry Industry, Inc.**

SWEET AND SPICY CHICKEN STIR-FRY

1 can (8 ounces) DEL MONTE®
    Pineapple Chunks in Its
    Own Juice
1 tablespoon vegetable oil
1 boneless skinless chicken
    breast, cubed
    Salt and pepper (optional)

¼ to ½ teaspoon crushed red
    pepper flakes or hot pepper
    sauce
1 can (16 ounces) DEL MONTE®
    Blue Lake Cut Green Beans,
    drained
¾ cup sweet and sour sauce*
    Hot cooked rice (optional)

Drain pineapple, reserving ¼ cup juice. In 10 to 12-inch wok or skillet, heat oil over medium heat. Add chicken; cook and stir 5 minutes. Season with salt and pepper, if desired. Stir in reserved ¼ cup juice and red pepper flakes. Reduce heat; cook, uncovered, 2 minutes. Add green beans, pineapple and sauce. Cover; cook 2 minutes or until heated through. Serve over hot cooked rice, if desired. *Makes 4 servings*

Total time: 20 minutes

*Helpful Hint: Sweet and sour sauce is available in international section of supermarket. *Or* combine ½ cup water, ¼ cup granulated sugar, 3 tablespoons cider vinegar, 3 tablespoons DEL MONTE® Ketchup and 4 teaspoons cornstarch. Cook, stirring constantly, until thickened and translucent.

SWEET CHICKEN RISOTTO

1 tablespoon vegetable oil
¾ pound boneless skinless
    chicken breasts, thinly
    sliced
¾ cup onion, chopped
4 cups chicken broth *or* 2 cans
    (14 ounces *each*) chicken
    broth
2 cups uncooked instant brown
    rice

1 tablespoon prepared
    horseradish
4 teaspoons sugar
14 ounces canned black beans,
    rinsed and drained *or*
    2 cups cooked beans
1 medium green bell pepper,
    sliced
1 medium red bell pepper, sliced
¼ cup grated Parmesan cheese

Heat oil in 3 to 4-quart saucepan over medium-high heat. Add chicken and onion; cook 5 minutes, turning to brown both sides. Add chicken broth, rice, horseradish and sugar. Reduce heat to low. Cover and simmer 15 minutes or until rice is tender. (There should be extra liquid.) Add beans and peppers. Simmer 5 minutes. Sprinkle with cheese before serving.

Makes 4 servings

Favorite recipe from **The Sugar Association, Inc.**

CARIBBEAN CHICKEN PAELLA

1 large clove garlic, minced
1 teaspoon dried oregano
  leaves, crushed
6 COOKIN' GOOD® Drumsticks
  and Thighs
2 tablespoons red wine vinegar
1 tablespoon olive oil
½ pound ham, chopped
1 large green pepper, chopped

1 medium onion, chopped
2 large tomatoes, cored and
  chopped
6 cups chicken broth
2 cups uncooked rice
1 cup frozen peas, thawed
¼ cup pimento-stuffed green
  olives
1 tablespoon capers

1. In small bowl, combine garlic and oregano; coat chicken. Place chicken in shallow dish; sprinkle with vinegar. Cover and refrigerate 1 hour.

2. In 5-quart Dutch oven over medium heat, heat oil. Cook chicken about 15 minutes, browning on all sides. Remove chicken to plate.

3. In drippings in Dutch oven over medium heat, cook ham, green pepper and onion 10 minutes or until tender, stirring occasionally. Add tomatoes; cook 5 minutes, stirring frequently. Add broth, rice and chicken. Bring to a boil over high heat.

4. Reduce heat to low. Cover; simmer 25 minutes. Stir in peas, olives and capers; heat through. *Makes 4 servings*

TAMALE PIE

1 cup yellow cornmeal
½ cup all-purpose flour
1 teaspoon DAVIS® Baking
  Powder
1 cup water
2 cups shredded Cheddar
  cheese (8 ounces), divided

1 egg, beaten
1 pound chopped cooked
  chicken
1 (12-ounce) jar ORTEGA® Mild,
  Medium or Hot Thick and
  Chunky Salsa
½ cup sliced pitted ripe olives

In medium bowl, blend cornmeal, flour and baking powder; stir in water, 1 cup cheese and egg. Spread half the cornmeal mixture on bottom of greased 9-inch pie plate; set aside.

In medium bowl, combine chicken, salsa and ½ cup cheese; spoon into prepared pie plate. Spoon remaining cornmeal mixture over chicken mixture to within 1 inch of plate edge. Bake at 350°F for 35 minutes or until top is golden brown. Top with remaining cheese and olives; bake 5 minutes more or until cheese melts. *Makes 6 to 8 servings*

Prep time: 20 minutes   **Cook time:** 40 minutes

Caribbean Chicken Paella

MEXICAN LASAGNA

2 tablespoons vegetable oil
1½ tablespoons chili powder
1½ pounds COOKIN' GOOD®
    Boneless Skinless Chicken
    Breasts *or* COOKIN' GOOD®
    Boneless Skinless Chicken
    Thighs, cut into 1-inch
    pieces
½ teaspoon salt, divided
1 large onion, diced
1 can (4 ounces) chopped green
    chili peppers, drained
2 teaspoons ground cumin

1 can (28 ounces) tomatoes,
    drained and chopped
1 can (15 to 16 ounces) pinto
    beans, drained and rinsed
1 container (15 ounces) light
    ricotta cheese
2 egg whites
2 cups (8 ounces) shredded
    Monterey Jack cheese with
    jalapeño peppers, divided
1 package corn tortillas (12 per
    package)

1. Preheat oven to 375°F. In 10-inch skillet combine oil and chili powder; cook 1 minute over medium heat. Increase heat to medium-high. Add half the chicken pieces and ¼ teaspoon salt. Cook 4 minutes, stirring frequently. Remove chicken to large bowl with slotted spoon. Repeat with remaining chicken and ¼ teaspoon salt. Remove chicken. Cook in drippings remaining in skillet, onion, chili peppers and cumin 5 minutes, stirring frequently. Spoon onion mixture into bowl with chicken. Add tomatoes and beans.

2. Combine ricotta cheese, egg whites and 1 cup Monterey Jack cheese in separate bowl.

3. Line bottom and sides of greased 3-quart round, shallow casserole or baking dish with 8 tortillas. Spoon about ⅔ chicken mixture into casserole. Cover with cheese mixture. Arrange remaining tortillas on top of cheese mixture. Spoon remaining chicken mixture on top. Sprinkle with remaining 1 cup Monterey Jack cheese. Bake 35 minutes or until heated through. *Makes 6 to 8 servings*

CHICKEN FAJITAS

¼ cup REGINA® Red Wine
    Vinegar
¼ cup vegetable oil, divided
2 tablespoons A.1.® Steak
    Sauce
2 teaspoons WRIGHT'S®
    Natural Hickory Seasoning
½ teaspoon liquid hot pepper
    seasoning

1 pound boneless skinless
    chicken breasts, cut into
    strips
1 large green pepper, cut into
    strips
1 large onion, cut into wedges
8 flour tortillas, heated
    Sour cream and shredded
        Cheddar cheese, for garnish

Blend vinegar, 2 tablespoons oil, steak sauce, hickory seasoning and hot pepper seasoning. In nonmetal bowl, pour marinade over chicken. Cover; chill for 1 to 2 hours, stirring occasionally. Drain chicken.

In large skillet, over medium-high heat, cook green pepper and onion in remaining 2 tablespoons oil for 5 to 6 minutes or until tender. Remove from skillet with slotted spoon; set aside. In same skillet, cook and stir chicken for 10 to 12 minutes or until no longer pink. Add reserved peppers and onions; cook for 3 to 5 minutes more or until heated through.

Serve hot with tortillas; garnish with sour cream and cheese.

Makes 4 servings

CHICKEN JAMBALAYA

2 cups chicken broth
1 can (14½ ounces) tomatoes, chopped, reserve liquid
1 can (8 ounces) tomato sauce
½ cup finely chopped onions
¼ cup chopped green pepper
½ teaspoon dried basil leaves, crushed
½ teaspoon dried thyme leaves, crushed

1 bay leaf
1 cup uncooked converted rice
1 cup KELLOGG'S® ALL-BRAN® cereal
8 ounces smoked turkey sausage, sliced
3 cups chopped cooked chicken
2 tablespoons chopped parsley

1. In 4-quart saucepan, place chicken broth, tomato liquid, tomato sauce, onions, green pepper and seasonings. Cook over medium heat until mixture boils, stirring occasionally.

2. Stir in tomatoes, rice, Kellogg's® All-Bran® cereal and turkey sausage. Cover pan and cook over medium heat until mixture starts to boil. Stir in chicken. Reduce heat. Cover and simmer 25 minutes or until moisture is absorbed and rice is cooked.

3. Remove bay leaf and stir in parsley. Serve hot.

Makes 9 cups, 6 servings

Chicken Rellenos

CHICKEN RELLENOS

8 small poblano or green bell peppers (about 2 ounces *each*)
1 can (8½ ounces) whole kernel corn, drained
2 cans (4 ounces *each*) chunk white chicken, drained
1 can (4 ounces) sliced mushrooms, drained

1 cup (4 ounces) shredded Monterey Jack cheese
2 tablespoons chopped pimiento
1 or 2 canned jalapeño peppers, finely chopped
1 clove garlic, minced
1 tablespoon vegetable oil

Remove tops from poblano peppers; scoop out and discard seeds. Mix corn, chicken, mushrooms, cheese, pimiento, jalapeño peppers and garlic; spoon mixture into poblano peppers. Heat oil in large skillet over medium-high heat; cook peppers, browning all sides. Reduce heat to low. Cover; cook, turning occasionally, until peppers are tender, 5 to 10 minutes.

Makes 4 servings

Favorite recipe from **Canned Food Information Council**

CHICKEN PICADILLO

1 can (16 ounces) whole
   tomatoes, chopped
½ cup golden raisins
1 tablespoon chopped green
   chilies
1 teaspoon sugar
1 teaspoon ground cinnamon
½ teaspoon salt

½ teaspoon ground cumin
⅛ teaspoon ground red pepper
2 tablespoons vegetable oil
8 skinless broiler-fryer chicken
   thighs
½ cup chopped onion
   Hot cooked rice
¼ cup sliced almonds

Mix together tomatoes, raisins, chilies, sugar, cinnamon, salt, cumin and red pepper in small bowl; set aside. Heat oil in large skillet over medium-high heat. Add chicken and cook, turning to brown all sides, about 10 minutes. Cook and stir onion 2 to 3 minutes until soft. Drain off excess fat. Add tomato mixture. Reduce heat to medium. Cover; cook about 15 minutes or until chicken is fork-tender. Uncover; cook 5 minutes longer. Serve chicken and sauce over hot cooked rice. Sprinkle with almonds.

Makes 4 servings

Favorite recipe from **Delmarva Poultry Industry, Inc.**

DREAMY CREAMY CHICKEN LASAGNA

½ of a (1-pound) package
   CREAMETTE® Lasagna,
   uncooked
1 (12-ounce) can evaporated
   milk
2 tablespoons cornstarch
2 cups chicken broth
½ cup grated Parmesan cheese
¼ cup white wine
2 tablespoons Dijon-style
   mustard
2 teaspoons tomato sauce

2 cloves garlic, minced
½ teaspoon dried basil leaves,
   crushed
¼ teaspoon ground nutmeg
⅛ teaspoon ground red pepper
2 cups cooked chicken, torn into
   small pieces
6 cherry tomatoes, sliced into
   thin wedges
1 cup (4 ounces) shredded
   American cheese
   Hungarian sweet paprika

Prepare Creamette® Lasagna according to package directions; drain. In large saucepan, blend together evaporated milk and cornstarch. Whisk in chicken broth, Parmesan cheese, wine, mustard, tomato sauce, garlic, basil, nutmeg and red pepper. Bring to a boil, stirring until thickened and bubbly. Remove from heat. Reserve 1¼ cups. Stir chicken and tomatoes into remaining sauce. Into a 13×9-inch baking dish, spoon ¼ cup reserved sauce. Layer ⅓ the lasagna and half the chicken sauce. Repeat, ending with Lasagna. Spread on remaining 1 cup sauce. Top with cheese and paprika. Bake, covered, in 350°F oven 35 to 40 minutes. Let stand 10 minutes before cutting. Refrigerate leftovers.

Makes 8 to 10 servings

CHICKEN MANICOTTI WITH WINE SAUCE

8 dry PASTA DeFINO® No Boil®
Lasagna Noodles
1 pound boneless skinless
chicken breasts, halved
1 tablespoon olive or
vegetable oil
4 ounces fresh mushrooms,
sliced

½ cup sliced green onions
1 cup light sour cream
1 cup shredded reduced-fat
Swiss cheese
1 jar (23.5 ounces) simmering
sauce for Herbed Chicken
with Wine

Soak lasagna noodles in hot tap water 8 to 10 minutes or until softened, taking care noodles do not stick together. Cut chicken into bite-size pieces. Heat oil in nonstick 10-inch skillet over medium-high heat; cook and stir chicken, mushrooms and onions until chicken is lightly browned. Cool slightly. Stir in sour cream and Swiss cheese.

Cut each softened noodle in half, making 16 squares, 4 inches each. Spray 13×9×2-inch glass baking dish with nonstick cooking spray. Divide chicken mixture equally among softened noodles; roll-up. Place seam side down into baking dish. Pour sauce over rolled noodles.

Cover baking dish with foil. Bake in 400°F oven 15 minutes. Uncover and bake 10 to 15 minutes longer. Let stand 5 minutes before cutting.

Makes 8 servings

MICROWAVE DIRECTIONS: Cover glass dish of sauced rolled noodles with plastic wrap. Cook on HIGH (100% power) 15 to 18 minutes, turning dish twice during cooking. Let stand 5 minutes before cutting.

CHICKEN OLÉ

2 boneless skinless chicken
breasts, halved
1 (12-ounce) jar ORTEGA® Mild,
Medium or Hot Thick and
Chunky Salsa

1 cup shredded Cheddar
cheese (4 ounces)
Parsley sprigs, for garnish

Arrange chicken breasts in 12×8×2-inch baking pan. Bake at 350°F for 15 minutes; drain if necessary. Spoon salsa over chicken; top with cheese. Bake 20 minutes more or until chicken is done. Garnish with parsley if desired.

Makes 4 servings

Prep time: 5 minutes   **Cook time:** 35 minutes

Thai-Style Chicken Curry

THAI-STYLE CHICKEN CURRY

1 can (20 ounces) DOLE®
   Pineapple Chunks in Syrup*
¼ cup peanut oil, divided
1 pound boneless skinless
   chicken breasts, chunked
1 pound eggplant, diced
1 medium yellow onion, diced
1 *each* DOLE® Green and Red
   Bell Pepper, seeded, diced

2 large cloves garlic, pressed
1 tablespoon curry powder
1 teaspoon salt
½ teaspoon ground cumin
¼ teaspoon *each* ground cloves,
   ground red pepper
1 cup canned coconut milk
2 teaspoons minced cilantro
2 cups hot cooked rice

• Drain pineapple; reserve syrup.

• In 8-inch nonstick skillet heat 1 tablespoon oil over medium-high heat; brown chicken, turning once. Remove from skillet.

• In same skillet heat remaining 3 tablespoons oil over medium-high heat. Cook eggplant until light brown (expect a little sticking). Add onion. Cover; cook 1 minute. Add green and red bell peppers, garlic, curry, salt, cumin, cloves and ground red pepper. Cook, uncovered, until slightly softened.

• Stir in reserved pineapple juice with coconut milk. Blend well, scraping brown particles from bottom of skillet. Reduce heat to low. Cover; simmer 30 minutes.

• Uncover and add chicken; simmer 15 minutes longer. Stir in pineapple and cilantro; heat through. Serve with rice. *Makes 4 servings*

*Use pineapple packed in juice if desired.

Prep time: 20 minutes   **Cook time:** 50 minutes

Fried Rice

FRIED RICE

1 cup MJB/FARMHOUSE®
    Original Long Grain White
    Rice
2 tablespoons vegetable oil,
    divided
2 eggs, beaten

½ cup finely diced boneless
    skinless chicken breast,
    uncooked
½ cup finely diced smoked ham
¼ cup finely diced carrots
½ cup frozen peas, thawed
¼ cup thinly sliced green onions
3 tablespoons soy sauce

Prepare rice according to package directions (omitting butter and salt).
Meanwhile, heat 1 tablespoon oil in large skillet over medium-high heat.
Cook eggs, breaking up with a fork; set aside. Cook chicken, ham and
carrots in same skillet in remaining 1 tablespoon oil 5 to 7 minutes or until
chicken is cooked. Add cooked rice, peas, green onions and soy sauce. Stir
until well blended and heated through. *Makes 6 cups*

NEW DELHI CHICKEN THIGHS

8 skinless broiler-fryer chicken
    thighs
1 cup plain yogurt
¼ cup mango chutney
2 cloves garlic, halved
    ½-inch piece ginger root
1 tablespoon vinegar

1 tablespoon chopped cilantro
1 teaspoon curry powder
1 teaspoon paprika
1 teaspoon salt
½ teaspoon ground cumin
¼ teaspoon ground red pepper

Arrange chicken in single layer in shallow baking pan. Combine in blender container, yogurt, chutney, garlic, ginger root, vinegar, cilantro, curry powder, paprika, salt, cumin and red pepper; process until smooth. Pour yogurt sauce over chicken, turning pieces to coat all sides. Cover; marinate in refrigerator at least 1 hour, turning chicken occasionally. Bake, basting several times, in 400°F oven 45 to 50 minutes until chicken is brown and fork-tender. *Makes 4 servings*

Favorite recipe from **Delmarva Poultry Industry, Inc.**

GREEN CHILE CHICKEN

1 pound boneless skinless
    chicken breasts, cut into
    thin strips
1 medium onion, sliced
1 clove garlic, crushed
2 tablespoons vegetable oil
1 (12-ounce) jar ORTEGA® Mild
    Thick and Chunky Salsa

1 (4-ounce) can ORTEGA® Diced
    Green Chiles
½ teaspoon dried oregano
    leaves, crushed
Hot cooked rice or flour
    tortillas
Dairy sour cream (optional)

In medium skillet, over medium-high heat, cook chicken, onion and garlic in oil until chicken is no longer pink. Add salsa, chiles and oregano. Simmer, uncovered, 10 minutes. Serve over rice with sour cream, if desired.
Makes 6 servings

ROMANCE® CHICKEN MARINARA

1 tablespoon olive oil
¾ pound boneless skinless
    chicken breasts, halved, cut
    into ½-inch strips
1 cup red and/or green bell
    pepper strips

1 medium zucchini, thinly sliced
    (about 1 cup)
1 package (7 ounces)
    ROMANCE® Marinara Sauce
1 package (12 ounces)
    ROMANCE® Linguine

Heat oil in large nonstick skillet over medium heat. Cook chicken, stirring occasionally, until chicken is no longer pink, about 4 minutes. Remove from skillet. Cook peppers and zucchini in same skillet 3 minutes or until crisp-tender. Return chicken to skillet with vegetables; add Marinara Sauce. Reduce heat to low. Cover; simmer 5 minutes. Meanwhile, prepare linguine as directed on package. Serve chicken mixture spooned over linguine.
Makes 4 servings

ACKNOWLEDGMENTS

*The publishers would like to thank the companies and organizations
listed below for the use of their recipes in this publication.*

Bel Paese Sales Company
Bongrain Cheese U.S.A.
California Date Administrative
  Committee
California Table Grape Commission
Canned Food Information Council
Checkerboard Kitchens, Ralston
  Purina Company
Chef Paul Prudhomme's Magic
  Seasoning Blends™
Chilean Fresh Fruit Association
Cookin' Good
The Creamette Company
Delmarva Poultry Industry, Inc.
Del Monte Foods

Dole Food Company, Inc.
Kellogg Company
Thomas J. Lipton Co.
M.J.B. Rice Company
Nabisco Foods Group
National Dairy Board
Nestlé Food Company
Pecan Marketing Board
Perdue Farms
Pet Incorporated
Romance Foods, Inc.
Shade Pasta
The Sugar Association, Inc.
Wampler-Longacre, Inc.
Washington Apple Commission

PHOTO CREDITS

*The publishers would like to thank the companies and organizations
listed below for the use of their photographs in this publication.*

Bel Paese Sales Company
Bongrain Cheese U.S.A.
California Date Administrative
  Committee
Canned Food Information Council
Cookin' Good
The Creamette Company
Delmarva Poultry Industry, Inc.

Dole Food Company, Inc.
M.J.B. Rice Company
National Dairy Board
Nestlé Food Company
Pecan Marketing Board
The Sugar Association, Inc.
Washington Apple Commission

INDEX